A Fashion Retailer's Guide to Thriving in Turbulent Times

By raising questions and providing scenarios for success, this book embraces fashion brand development in current turbulent retail environments. A brand must have an essence; it needs to respect a philosophy, abide by values and follow clear processes. A brand's success and sustainability follow specific rules, nonetheless for fashion brands. But do fashion brand management rules apply in today's turbulent times? Acknowledging and going beyond branding theory, this book challenges knowledge and practices that have been guiding fashion retail brands for many years. Co-written by an academic researcher and a retail consultant with 30 years of experience, this practical guide offers not a process that fashion brands must follow, but potential avenues for survival in today's retail market and facing today's customers. Professionals and students of fashion retailing and branding will appreciate the detailed case studies that illustrate revisited concepts and thought-provoking suggestions on how to make decisions for an uncertain future.

Ghalia Boustani is a researcher at Paris 1 Panthéon Sorbonne, France, and holds a doctorate from Ecole Supérieure des Affaires, Lebanon. Her main research interest is in ephemeral retailing; after completing her first study on pop-up stores in the Middle East, she has now focused her research on pop-up stores in Europe. Throughout her academic journey, Ghalia has also worked closely with professionals and entrepreneurs on several projects that added value to her research.

Daniela Leonini brings 30 years of experience in interior design and fashion to her work as a senior retail consultant, advising start-ups and conglomerates alike on issues such as retail stores, team recruitment and training, and merchandising. Before opening her own consultancy, Daniela had management roles at the Paris-based store Merci and Sézane, the first French online brand. Beyond her strategy and marketing work, she also designs home décor objects, fabrics, furniture and lamps.

"The book explores strategies open to fashion brands to achieve success and longevity in the vastly changing world of retail. The author draws on her wealth of experience to focus on 'doing the right things'" as opposed to the line manager's conventional approach of perfecting tactics in order to 'do things right'." The insight and advice it contains will be useful not only to academics striving to update retail and brand management texts but also to managers facing the challenge of operating in an ever more challenging environment. The authors' purpose is to explore what added value a physical retail store can offer as part of today's shopping journey. This means not only re-evaluating the essence of what the brand itself stands for but also how this is manifested in terms of the retail format proposition and experience. The way forward is no longer generic but optimized for each brand and involves many qualities including differentiation, stimulation, relevance and agility. The author examines various levels in the marketplace but concludes that the boundaries between these levels are increasingly blurred. A highly recommended read."

—Bill Webb, Associate Lecturer, London College of Fashion, UK;
Member of The Ebeltoft Group of Global Retail & Branding Experts

"The retail industry has evolved in tandem with human development, from ancient markets through modern brick and mortar stores and, more recently, the internet-based virtual space. The fashion retail sector, as well as the socio-cultural framework in which it operates, has faced unprecedented challenges in the past two decades, not least from globalization, so-called 'democratization' and sustainability considerations, necessitating thorough-going reform. The industry now stands at a critical juncture as it tries to balance competing demands for stability, adaptability, sustainability, tech innovation and financial viability, not least in the wake of the coronavirus crisis. The authors' book on the fashion retail industry is particularly timely. The book adopts an 'unconformist angle' to approach the fashion retail industry, and this not only helps the reader build a valuable knowledge base on fashion retail, but also encourages the reader to reflect on a diverse range of contemporary issues the industry is currently encountering. It is an essential read for those who wish to study the field and establish a professional path in the retail fashion industry."

—Dr. Kelly Meng Goldsmiths, University of London, UK

A Fashion Retailer's Guide to Thriving in Turbulent Times

Ghalia Boustani and
Daniela Leonini

Routledge
Taylor & Francis Group

NEW YORK AND LONDON

Cover image: Getty

First published 2023
by Routledge
605 Third Avenue, New York, NY 10158

and by Routledge
4 Park Square, Milton Park, Abingdon, Oxon, OX14 4RN

Routledge is an imprint of the Taylor & Francis Group, an informa business

© 2023 Ghalia Boustani and Daniela Leonini

The right of Ghalia Boustani and Daniela Leonini to be identified as authors of this work has been asserted in accordance with sections 77 and 78 of the Copyright, Designs and Patents Act 1988.

ISBN: 978-1-032-00226-2 (hbk)
ISBN: 978-1-032-00225-5 (pbk)
ISBN: 978-1-003-17321-2 (ebk)

DOI: 10.4324/9781003173212

Typeset in Bembo
by Apex CoVantage, LLC

This book's content is a reflection of our academic and professional experiences.

We have both been fascinated by the fashion retail industry and have had the chance to work in or take part in different brand-related functions, their management and operationalization.

We have witnessed retail's development; as consumers and professionals.

We have been observing the retail environment and raising many management-related questions.

We would like to share our points of view with you as it is about time to rethink the way we are managing and guiding retail brands.

We take the opportunity to say thank you!

Thank you to each and everyone who contributed to making this book a success.

Thank you to each and every brand manager, entrepreneur and retail professional who have given us their valuable time to share valuable insights and knowledge about their brands.

We dedicate this book to those who, like us, love retail and pursue their efforts to make retail brands a success.

Contents

Ghalia Boustani

Ghalia Boustani is an academic lecturer and researcher. She holds a doctorate degree from Ecole Supérieure des affaires (ESA business school) and another from Paris 1 Panthéon Sorbonne. Her main research interest is in ephemeral retailing; she has developed her first research on pop-up stores in the Middle East and has focused her second research on studying different types of pop-up stores in Europe. Ghalia has published "Ephemeral Retailing: Pop-up stores in a postmodern consumption era", "Pop-up retail: the evolution, application and future of pop-up stores" and presented her research in different marketing and retailing colloquy.

Ghalia also worked closely with professionals and entrepreneurs on several projects that added value to her research. Professional projects paid much attention to developing entrepreneurial fashion brands. Other projects looked at analyzing, revising and implementing developed brand collection architectures, as well as physical visual merchandising strategies. Another aspect looked at collaborating with brands to work on specific retail and marketing content to be shared on their social media outlets.

Since 2014, Ghalia has been developing considerable online content that looks at retailing in general, ephemeral retailing in particular, the fashion business and the fashion retail industry. This curated content is shared on different social media channels: blogs, illustrations, recorded videos and live chats.

Daniela Leonini

Daniela Leonini is a retail consultant whose area of expertise is customer experience.

She has been working with fashion, design and lifestyle brands for more than 30 years. The scope of work varied from wholesale to retail, from interior design to brand management. Her main clients were Yves Saint Laurent, Sonia Rykiel, Cacharel, Merci, Sézane and Made.com.

In 2019, Daniela creates her agency Appuntamento. She accompanies her clients to implement new omnichannel retail methods, to animate their physical or digital touchpoints and create experiences (places, teams, processes) by infusing emotion and care.

Daniela also teaches in various business schools: ESSEC, EM Normandie and Institute Paul Bocuse.

About this book

This book reflects our vision of fashion retail brands and their management. We have condensed several years of experience and reflections into several pages, to share our point of view on management-related matters. We have also spoken with brand managers, designers and retail professionals to understand the realities of the retail environment as we believe that qualitative data help highlight emerging variables that reflect most the state of the market under investigation.

A total of 25 semi-directive interviews have been collected between March 2021 and September 2021. Data was collected from the French and the Lebanese markets.

The sample consisted of French and Lebanese brands that are at entrepreneurial or developed brand stages. The areas of activities range from fashion accessories (jewelry and handbags) to garments (ready-to-wear, customized or couture).

After having taken the permission to record the interview, all content has been saved in respective folders, fully transcribed and prepared for analysis.

Naturally, academic and professional sources set the basis of this books content.

Our aim is not to re-invent knowledge or pretend to do so. Our aim, on one hand, is to present our understanding of the current retail market's reading. On the other hand, we aim to provide suggestions that invite managers/professionals to look at the situation related to managing their brands, or making decisions related to their brands, differently.

Table 0.1 List of interviewed fashion brands

Brand	Establishment	Manager	Origin	Description
Maison Percée	2020	Julie Dargent	France	An artist's edition house where art and object become one. The concept consists of marrying an artist with an artisan to conceive and produces exclusive objects that transmit their creator's values.
Absolution	2008	Isabelle Carron	France	Organic and customizable cosmetics and skin care that are made in France.
Boks & Baum	2014	Sylvie Boksenbaum	France	Anything but minimalistic fashion jewelry that is made of threads and stones, but not metal.
Cho Konzept	2019	Tanja Heiss	France	Affordable Fairtrade jewelry.
Claire Dartrigue	2017	Claire Dartigue	France	Upcycling and transformation studio. A blend between sports, couture and art.
Do Paris	2009	Dorothée Groneskoul	France	Women woven one-piece swimsuits and other jersey items.
Entremains	2019	Camille Chatelet et Sophie Boirard	France	A curation of previously owned pieces that are acquired, reconditioned and re-sold.
France XXI	2013	Guillaume Combemorel	France	A brand that proudly bears the name of "France" and stands for cultural aspects related to the country. It locally sources and produces.
Hello Elae	2019	Ezgi Samioglu	France	A transparent baby fashion brand that focuses on product functionality and that is produced in reduce quantities. Its model consists of engaging women and creating employment opportunities. The unisex, evolving and eco-friendly changing room for a new generation of babies.

(Continued)

Table 0.1 (Continued)

Brand	Establishment	Manager	Origin	Description
Nathalie Lacroix		Nathalie Lacroix		A showroom in which emerging talents are revealed and innovative ideas refined. The concept advocates collaborating with artisans or brands that transmit meaning and value through their work.
Nicholas Villani	1960	Jeanne et Emma Villani		High-end ready-to-wear fashion brand that caters to women and men. The brand develops pieces with unique details and finishing and that rarely go out of fashion.
Point physique	2020	Noémie Pauquet		Multi-brand themed physical pop-up stores putting together designers and brands.
Token Monde	2016	Marie Figueredo		The brand's ethos relates around the vest. Since it is the last item that one puts on, the vest could transmit a lot about who the person is and what statement he is making.
White bird	2010	Stéphanie Roger		High-end unique jewelry brands that women can purchase several times per year. This precious piece can accompany a woman throughout her journey and can be offered or transmitted.
Heureux Les Curieux	2018	Sabrina Piperno		A meeting place in the Haut Marais between brands and consumers where experience is the key because it awakens the senses and gives meaning to consumption. More than a pop-up, HEUREUX LES CURIEUX is a sustainable place.
Atelier Particulier	2013	Fulbert Lecoq		French digital native vertical brands which sells fashion accessories and ready-to-wear on the Internet, under their own brand Atelier Particulier with a unique positioning on the market which is to find and reveal know-how.

Tony Ward Couture	1997	Youmna Assouad	Made to measure luxury evening and bridal wear. Delicately cut, sewn and finished in Lebanon and shipped to high-end retailers and consumers worldwide.
Fore and Aft	2014	Charbel Feghaly	Selected men's wear fashion catering to those to appreciate quality, style and a personalized styling experience.
Azzi & Osta	2004	Georges Azzi &Assad Osta	Impeccable patterns, quality fabric and unique product finishing. Azzi & Osta's collections are conceived for those who value timeless fashion.
Taghrid el Hage	2008	Taghrid el Hage	Customized wedding and evening dresses. For women who look for a touch of romanticism, femininity and a sense of freedom.
Rawan Sleiman	2015	Rawan Sleiman	Craftsmanship in its purest form. Following know-how that was passed along from father to daughter, all made-to-order items were unique in their own rights.
Thalie Paris	2020	Nathalie Dionne	Brand of handbags and accessories with an innovative business model placed under the sign of the R&D, so much in the manners to conceive the collections that the research of new sustainable and responsible materials.

Book idea

We are certainly going to cross paths with someone, somewhere and at a certain point in time.

Our awareness and readiness could allow us to embrace that moment and turn this encounter into a meaningful event.

Whether we have all reached that state of mind, I can't tell; as far as I am concerned, every encounter is an opportunity that awaits to be cultivated, nurtured or abandoned.

Ghalia Boustani

Meeting people.

What's the significance of a meeting if it was a micro encounter? If it didn't last? If it grew into beautiful relationships? I cannot recall how many people I have met. But what I know for sure is that many have taught me, very few marked me and the greater majority disappointed me. Yes, every meeting has contributed to growing and shaping my experience.

When I meet someone, I pay much attention to his story, his/her point of view and his likes and dislikes. I also get inspired by his/her perspective on something or attitude toward someone. Whether personal, professional or accidental, these encounters have greatly contributed to widening my perspective and vision.

As much as the journey had been full of hope, it had been full of disappointments; but not in a disappointing way! I cannot count the number of times I have been let down by people whom I highly thought of or whom I have trusted. To all those who disappointed me, thank you. You made me realize that there is always a brighter side to look at.

This book reflects two decades of academic knowledge, professional experiences, a lookout on the retail environment and meaningful exchange with marketing and retail professionals. I met Daniela along the way; here we are, putting forward this book and sharing it with all of you!

Daniela Leonini

Writing a fashion retail book right after having witnessed a global retail recess . . . this has never occurred to me and would have never thought of experiencing. I was hoping to share some key elements that could be useful to retail managers and students, and the opportunity of this book presented itself.

It all started with a meeting.

The story of a meeting with Ghalia during these strange and turbulent times; our meeting happened over *Instagram*. When She suggested I participate in one of her Instagram Live sessions, it was a professional "love at first sight". Our relationship was nurtured with both our goodwill and approach toward our jobs: two paths, two complementary backgrounds joining course.

I have never written a book in my life; however, I am very passionate about fashion retail to the extent that it kindles my spirits and cultivates my passion for thinking and sharing about the topic. Venturing on this journey with Ghalia, who is used to this kind of exercise, is reassuring. This topic speaks to us as it is lively, dynamic and full of passion.

My career path made sense a few years ago when I realized that all I had experienced during my professional career, revolved around the retail business. I had been through so many different jobs, from design to sales and communication; all of which revolved around fashion and lifestyle. I realize today that my love and curiosity for retail give me a relentless drive to learn and keep improving my methods. Retail never sleeps and is never at rest. Every hour is different, every moment in the store is unique and every customer has something to tell us. One must love doing and undoing because there is always room for improvement. . . .

There are always discoveries to be made in retail.

There are always ships that we want to sail.

I want to tell you not how you should disembark. I want to advise you on how to keep your ship afloat during turbulent times.

Prologue

How did we come across the idea of the book?

Back in the year 2002, a couple of representatives set up an information kiosk at the university to introduce a student credit card. I find myself crossing the cafeteria to fill in an application and request a credit card. I thought to myself (and I hope that my mother would skip reading this part): this is a great way to shop for more and to try to explore online shopping. At least I would not have to ask mom for the money immediately.

I remember that the credit card was limited to 300 USD. But 300 is 300 and I surely had many plans to keep that amount turning to get the best out of that service. I take that card and go down to the computer lab; the internet was a "thing" at that time. "At least I would have a table internet connection", I said to myself, and then typed three words that meant a lot at the time and yet had so little significance to me: "(Fashion) Marketing Books".

Before I describe the shopping process and what happened later with my credit card, let me explain why I typed those exact three words.

I had a thing for shopping since a very young age. And like many kids, I might have got the fascination from my parents. But my dad hated the idea of *going shopping*. According to him, the act of purchase is based on a need that has to meet a specific objective, whether this objective is for a necessity purchase or a leisure purchase. What I could understand from my father at the time was that the act of shopping is seeking products or services that are meaningful, that serve a purpose and that are of use to us.

Mom, on the other hand, was more of a need-basis shopping woman who loved to take time to look for what she needed. I must admit, she had taste and she had the opportunity to shop differently. I accompanied mom to her morning fitting at a couturier's atelier, a trip to the mall, an afternoon at the department store, a stop at the supermarket and a walk on the high street. What I could learn from my mother at that time is that there is a price to pay for quality. I learned that quality is simple and minimalistic and that owning fewer, but qualitative items, is better than having too much of perishable items.

And then was my time. My time to discover retail in my own way and my at own pace. If I can describe this journey in one word, I would say "risk" in making a purchase and "risk" to access the process of a purchase.

Throughout the years, and especially my adolescence, I had questions to better understand the world of retail. Why do brands look that way? Why do I favor one over the other (even if my mother had told me that the quality of the other is better)? Why is the merchandise displayed differently in this store? Why is this sales representative not following up with me in this store? What is the purpose of the sales season? Why does this store play cool music and why does everyone have the same dress code in that store?

What intrigued me at the time is the fact that there were differences in what I observed back at home as opposed to what I managed to observe whenever I traveled. And believe me when I say that I took this matter very seriously. With travel and discoveries also came all interrogations related to the conformity of retail practices and then the uniqueness of other retail practices. The shopping mall, at the time, was more of a "copied/paste" retail format: we would know how to read floor signage, we would expect to find a food court, sometimes a movie theater, and we would know where the powder rooms would be located and how to access the parking lot. What was striking though are the differences that are highly noticeable on the high street and in local markets.

Istanbul, 1997. "Ghalia, stay close! Don't get lost please!" Of course, she would have to repeat that every two seconds because I didn't know where to start looking and what to look at. I was fascinated with all the products and the richness around me. The Grand Bazaar was an experiential journey. A thousand times bigger than the souks I visited in Tripoli, Byblos or Tyr! There was a different vibe, a different body language that the shop owners or keepers spoke; I am referring here to the body language. Although I could depict similarities in displaying merchandise or similarities of the type of goods, something was different, and I had to translate it.

At that time, many used to book organized visits to leather producers and artisans. Of course, I accompanied my parents to one of these sessions. Once we took our seats, we assisted to a show where selected pieces were modeled. Once the time was up, customers had access to all items in the showroom and then could purchase or customize them. "Now that's something", I thought to myself. It so cool to assist to a fashion show and then purchase everything you like directly.

Jordan, 1999. I was on a short holiday with my mother, sister and a friend. We met with a family friend whom we haven't seen for years. Baggy jeans and cropped tops were "the thing" at that time. My friend and I chose our outfits and went to find mom in the lobby. It didn't take long before doing a U-turn and changing our outfits as they "were not fit with the location where we are going". Indeed, the souk was very local and less open for visitors or tourists. Concerning the local (retail) environment and culture, it was sensible and prudent to blend in with the prevailing "entourage".

A sunny summer week in Greece in the year 2000. Back then, it was "a big deal" to purchase items that no one else would have access to back home. I remember the time spent on the high street with my friends to select the coolest items that would stand out. During that period, it was very common for people to travel to France, Italy, London or Spain for their seasonal shopping. For every item that I judged, I looked at what was new and different from what could be found back home. That was the right choice. At least, I could confidently say that I have got "European" styles that are not found back home.

By the time I was 16, the country where I lived was dusting off the remains of civil war. New malls were developing and many franchise brands were taking their place inside them. Let me describe the situation with my 16-year-old vocabulary: many stores were selling locally produced items that were of good quality. Then all those new French, English, Italian and Spanish brands set foot in the country. As opposed to the local offering, these brands displayed collections with more coherent items. I remember very well that I found it more convenient to purchase a *whole outfit* from one brand at times when I had to complete my outfit by shopping from different stores. With these newly settled brands, price tags were hung on absolutely every item. There was no room for negotiating prices, even if the invoice's amount was high. And finally, there was no way to buy on credit. If I could say one thing at that time, I can only say that I found my true love among franchised brands. I had recently discovered a brand that opened its first location in West Beirut.

Crossing from East to West Beirut had yet to be digested. Lebanese civil war scars were still slowly healing. But try reasoning with a 17-year-old! My mom and I embarked on an expedition that day. "Mom, this is the top brand. I saw this pair of jeans in the magazine and called in to ask if the style is available and the lady confirmed that it is but that the quantity is limited". After a long drive (only because mom drives so slowly that time would seem to have stopped), we reached the destination. My heart was beating when I took the stairs to go down to the store. Dimmed lights, loud music, a cool temperature and a beautiful interior. Some items were hanging up, others were folded, and there were shoes, bags and accessories. I was going to have a heart attack! I couldn't be content with the beautiful pair of jeans, and I had to complete the purchase with everything else that could be worn with it . . . and the rest is history.

It is not easy growing up with contradictions, especially when you are aware of them, and you get to confront them. Back to the pre-franchised retail market state in Beirut (and I insist that it is Beirut as the majority of franchised retail brands opened in the capital). These beautiful concepts were embraced by consumers who entrusted them with their money without question. So now all local production was considered in a lesser category than "any" other "foreign brand". Maybe it is because local brands failed to cope with the esthetic retail dimension, and managerial dimension, that much fascinated local consumers.

The quality of a hand-finished garment could be questioned when the choice came down to purchasing an item of a similar category but from a franchised brand. The worst thing is that for quite some time, consumers failed to differentiate between one foreign brand and the other. They also had the idea that all their offerings had the same quality and that their retail prices were justified. Was the perception of local consumers skewed? Did the adoption of foreign retail concepts overshadow local retail? Is it the fact that foreign retailers have been developing their retail concepts to sell more than the product and that the local market was stuck to bulk production?

Just imagine me having a debate with mom over that.

Imagine me having this debate with the moms of my friends over that.

Imagine me discussing that with my friends, and I leave the rest to you.

I also had the chance to travel at a young age with my parents. It is the context and then the form that one gets to notice at first. Elsewhere, retail was done differently to back home. Even the brands that I was much accustomed to back home presented something different in the country where I was visiting. The high street was different, and it had a different vibe. Malls were different, as much as I can remember because they had a different vibe. But what is that "vibe"? And why am I not able to understand it?

At that time, everything that we used to purchase from abroad (and I insist on "everything") was perceived as being valuable. For instance, a T-shirt coming from mass brands that I bought for a couple of dollars was perceived as a very valuable T-shirt as I got it from France or Italy. Many fashion boutiques, opening in the 90s and the beginnings of the years 2000 in Beirut, bought stock or *fin de saison* collections to re-sell them. Whether the collections they bought consisted of quality merchandise or not is not the question; what mattered is that consumers were willing to pay a price in relation to the country from which the collection was imported.

Traveling with the family was an eye-opener. Traveling for studies and work, on the other hand, contributed to focusing my retail orientation and took our "relationship" to the next level. I had the chance to work with franchised retail brands, department stores and start-up brands. I was lucky to learn about their methods, assist to store openings in different countries and learn about retail "from the inside". I also learned about retail practices and their applications in different contexts and with different individuals.

Back to that computer lab.

The search led me to a list of books about fashion, marketing and fashion marketing.

I felt proud of myself because I would learn about something that very few are acquainted with, and this was a one-way ticket to building my beautiful career in the field of fashion. I was hoping to find answers or proof that what I grew to learn about fashion the industry is not what the fashion retail field really is. I thought, at the time, that learning about theoretical concepts and applying them would be a great way to have successful retail operations.

Online shopping neophyte at the time, I remember reading that credit card number and verifying it for the hundredth time. Funny how that card was small and still managed to let me lose my way of finding information that needed to be filled when it only had so little info. Name, address, billing info . . . purchase done. "And I will choose the least expensive shipping option". I could save up on every dollar I can for my next selection of books; I thought to myself.

The first book on a new topic is always fun to read: you get to read it and understand the words and their significance without necessarily grasping the concept.

At least this is how I process things.

It is only after examining, confronting and processing the information that you get back to re-reading the book which content will make sense. The time between the first and second reading might not be short. Sometimes it takes months or even years.

Here am I, confronted with retail from a shopping, management and esthetic perspective. Having acquired a global overview helped to focus on the area in which I wanted to specialize. From the day I invested in that first book, my mission was to grow my academic knowledge in fashion retail on one hand and keep nurturing that knowledge through hands-on professional activities on the other.

The discrepancy between a textbook and the application of notions it provided was among the hardest tasks yet the most rewarding. The question that I wanted to answer was whether a reference fashion marketing or retailing book's content could be learned and then literally applied in any given market or context. By the time I started my first retail job, I was confronted with the "why? And why not?" situations. Most of the time, my manager's answer came out as follows: "because I said so", "stop asking many questions", "we have always done things this way, so there is no reason we change now". Some other times, I could get more satisfying answers like "because brand management sent us these guidelines" or "this reflects the brands' identity".

I have also had the chance to travel to several neighboring counties where companies I have been working for wanted to open different points of sale. I started noticing the little details that differed from one area to another and one country to another. There were very strong cultural and human aspects that could not be neglected and that seemed (most of the time) of greater importance than the "brand guidelines": an international brand, its international guidelines but with local applications. It took quite some time for me to realize that retail is about the brand, marketing and processes; but what really makes retail successful is the "human variable".

Around the fall of 2006 and after a long week of intensive floor work, we manage to meet the deadline of a store opening. I cannot deny the fact that my job was the *coolest*. I could brag that I was traveling every other week to a different country and that I was working in fashion. For a 23-year-old Middle Eastern young woman, I couldn't but feel proud of myself. This came however at a price; traveling to assist in a store opening, to foresee store opening, train foreign team members or oversee brand applications, was very demanding physically and mentally. It was also very challenging.

Many of my supervisors had been working in retail for many years. It was an accidental career, most of the time. Like many other young women, I took a part-time job during my studies. With my first job, I saw myself growing up to reaching managerial positions. This is an experience-based work skill, I thought to myself one day. What if it was coupled with specific academic knowledge? I kept reflecting on those books I keep buying and reading. I kept asking myself whether coupling knowledge and experience would make us better retail employees. My elder brother majored in engineering because he wanted to be a mechanical engineer and wants to work in that industry. So, why was it less comprehensible to people when I expressed my interest in specializing in fashion retail?

In the turmoil of growing up the ladder and taking a position with higher responsibilities or pursuing my academic path to specialize in retail studies, I decided to put my professional career on hold and reinvest in my education. I chose to move to London.

My shoes could bear witness to the number of times I walked on Oxford Street. Selfridges was my second home. I could count every single store on Carnaby street and revive my inspiration at Liberty. Kensington Highstreet? Portobello road market? Tottenham court road? Camden town? Been there. Done that. And for a thousand times. My vision of the London retail and shopping experience was different at that time as I got to see it from a retailer's perspective. Why is shopping in London different? What differentiates retail in London? Why do tourists come to shop in London and why are Londoners so fond of their retail experience? There was "something" that did not relate to the retail scene or the offering. At the time, I was discovering the world of consumption as an experience: The experience of acquisition, of the retail environment and all other variables that *positively* influence a retail environment.

I received an email about our thesis proposal and was very hesitant that afternoon; what would my proposal be about? I was interested in *vintage* shopping and the rise of *second-hand boutiques*. I thought it was something to look at closely and nurture in terms of retail concepts. But I had to drop that idea quickly because I *felt* at that time that the world was not ready to accept this kind of retail concept yet. Then I thought that it would be interesting to focus on the retail experience. However, I had a narrow angle of developing that topic from a customer or retailer perspective. I wanted to study experiences but from a retail perspective. . . . Call it a happy coincidence or not, I take the jubilee line the next morning and I grab a newspaper on the way into the tube. A headline about a *pop-up store* appearing in East London. "That's cool", I thought to myself. Got to go check it out. I cut out that article and filed it as soon as I got to my studio, I took my digital camera the next morning (yes, we still used those back then) and head down for an expedition. As I entered the pop-up store, I stood still. I secretly took as my photos as I could (because taking photos inside retail spaces was not very desirable at the time), hid my camera and stood still. Big space, no stock, the iconic brand product only showcased. One assistant standing close to his desk, and a security member was at the door. Empty spaces, themed décor, and an atmosphere to which I was not accustomed to.

The pop-up retail expedition had started, and the thesis proposal was soon to be written. I thought that it would be ideal to explore whether these stores could help fashion ventures (or start-ups) develop and grow while minimizing traditional bricks-and-mortar costs and maximizing brand visibility. My quest for pop-up stores never stopped since that day.

Back to the Middle East, and after a couple of years in London, it was time for me to move forward with my career path. This time, along with my boutique retail consulting agency, I started teaching at different universities and business schools. I might have been among the very few who studied strategic marketing and specialized in the fashion industry *at that time*. My aim was to share retail experiences that I had acquired and confront and discuss them with academic knowledge. The journey was not easy, and my teaching methods were not always welcome among fellow colleagues. Moreover, the ecosystem was not ready to provide an adequate fashion retail study environment. Nevertheless, I have managed to deliver different types of professional and academic fashion retail-related courses that blend theory and practice and through which I tried to incite students to develop their own critical thinking.

From an academic perspective, I was keen on delivering notions regarding the fashion business differently. This surely did not mean that the wheel had to be re-invented, but I wanted to deliver to my students a different way of looking, analyzing, interpreting and acting. Culture played an important role; students were still accustomed to practices that they have been exposed to from their local environment and inherited from their families. The concept of "brand, brand identity, culture, practices" was relatively new. Fashion was still much related to a seamstress who cuts and sews garments (and the designs were inspired from those on fashion magazine covers).

From a professional point of view, I *struggled* with many Middle Eastern start-ups and medium-sized fashion brands. They could only project their success to that of established global or luxury brands; this was their only point of reference. The gap between reality and aspiration was very wide. Therefore, keeping an eye on fashion and retail from a research perspective was a must; it would keep me updated, equipped with quality knowledge and not conforming to a local retail reality that was not rapidly coping with retail advances. The great accelerated retail development and the many changes resulting from it grabbed my attention. Moreover, it was interesting to proctor the wave moving from west to east. Given the nature of research, my area of study was restricted to retail formats and consumer behavior, and it focused on fashion retail.

After three years of research, I earned my Ph.D. 2017 from the ESA business school). I have focused my studies on pop-up retail formats, in the Middle Eastern markets, and their influence on consumer behavior. That same year, I took on a research contract at Paris 1 Panthéon Sorbonne and pursued further investigation with the same topic but concentrating on data collection on the French market and different pop-up store categories. A couple of years later, I started meeting academics and professionals, to discuss retail formats and retail environments, in a live format. The objective was to put forward quality retail content (and when possible, fashion retail content) in a conversational style to reach an important number of interested audiences. I like to look at these live chats as "thinking out loud", raising questions to raise more questions and aspiring at having more answers.

I have been actively working on ways to develop "digestible" content that is related to the fashion retail industry. This initiative dates to 2012 when I organized retail, developed workshops and started creating social media content among other activities. Later in 2017, the "Fashion Business", a 24-episode television program that reflects the state of the fashion business in the Middle East. It confronts the local market's reality of the local market and questions whether marketing, branding and retailing practices conform to those of international standards.

As social media platforms became an integral part of our daily lives, I saw the opportunity that they presented in terms of assuring presence, allowing exchange and providing the possibility to meet people with no limitation to time and geography. During the first wave of lockdown, I found myself isolated from my colleagues and less able to meet people and discuss about the industry. I did not re-invent the wheel or create an innovative concept; the idea behind "Live with Ghalia" was to meet professional and academics, on a regular basis, talk about retail and marketing topics that are of academic standards but delivered in a conversational style that speaks to the majority. These chats added the spontaneity and flavor to topics that could have been considered as *scary* or out of reach.

Retail is *people*. Retail is *customers*. Retail is *environment*. Above all, retail management remains *commonsense*. If brands don't have the adequate teams, it is very difficult for them to function properly. If those don't feel implicated with the brand, it is very difficult for it to function properly. If customers don't adhere with the brand and its people, then it will not function properly. If brands and customers don't fit in the retail environment, then there would be no proper function. The question of "fit and functionality" is becoming more difficult to answer these days because of customer and brand fragmentation. Is there a right way to proceed? Is there one way to start or develop?

I have met people from around the globe. *Literally.* I wouldn't have been able to do that *physically* or *traditionally* as the costs of doing so could have been out of reach. I saw myself learning, widening my horizons, looking at things from different perspectives and expanding my reach overseas. Throughout my usual searches form profiles whom I could possibly invite to the live chat, I discover that of *Daniela Leonini.* I prepared the introduction message and send it to her. During our first live chat, we both felt that there was a beautiful chemistry. It was the pure hazard that let us cross paths, but we were happy that we (e-) met. Daniela and I found many similarities in our take on retail in general and fashion retail more specifically.

How and why, with a different but similar background to Ghalia's, did I feel "caught up" at a certain point in my life wanting to be in direct contact with customers? Why did I develop such a fascination with the world of retail? I think that I have always been captivated by stores. Since early my childhood, and during all my trips to different cities around the world, retail was a discovery. I spent time in souks, malls, high streets and department stores. I loved the next-door grocer and the hometown baker. Going shopping was my hobby and my mission.

Learning about the history of brands, and going to the field to compare and analyze, also became a passion. I wanted to understand why the store in London is very different from that of Paris or that of Berlin. How is it different? How can I translate that different "feeling" that I am getting? If there is one moment that I recall that marked my journey, it was the "Grand Bazar". I am picking up that landmark, as Ghalia did because it had an important effect on me. I was 15 years old when I landed in beautiful Istanbul. It was a shocking observation to see the local market's energy: shops, shopkeepers, the competition between them, the offering, the local consumer and tourists. I fascinated by the way shopkeepers attended to tourists and how they approached them. I was shocked by the number of competing stores in their proximity: antiques, jewelry, gold and textiles . . . all next to one another, all with the same offering. Why choose one over the other? What guarantees do I have that I won't be "taken advantage of"? how do I know if I am getting the best deal? How could I forget how an antique dealer invites you to sit on a pile of carpets and offers you to drink coffee or tea, to make you feel comfortable with your purchase?

At that very moment, I understood the importance of hospitality in retail.

I saw how important to understand the customer and adapt to their needs and learn to meet their expectations.

I realized that retail cannot make sense without interactions and exchange.

I also understood that a customer is not a "walking wallet". He must be sought after, advised, helped and listened to. Each customer is a different individual; brands and storekeepers are to keep that in mind to offer personalized and unique services that best speak to them.

If anything, I learned from that trip to the "Grand Bazaar", it is customer-centricity. That event that I experienced more than 30 years ago has been at the heart of commerce since the dawn of times. Nothing makes more sense to managing fashion retail during these "turbulent times": connecting with customers and making their visits to the store unique and unforgettable experiences.

When Ghalia and I started working on this manuscript, we wanted to make it as "real and true" as we could. As I sat down with different fashion brand managers and founders, I had a great opportunity to learn and understand their brands and management practices. Each one displays different problem-solving skills and adopts different approaches to meeting their objectives. One narrative that everyone shares: looking for the best way to serve customer and delivering a positive experience.

Easier said than done, different brands have different capabilities to manage. Even though their ideals are to deliver personalized customer retail experiences, they are not always in position to do so. Well, this manuscript aims to provide answers to these questions and to help rethinking current fashion retail management practices. I believe that this will be a first step to advising on managing fashion brands during turbulent time . . . Ghalia and I are looking forward to learning more.

I was intrigued by Daniella's story at first and when I spent more time exchanging with her, I saw that there were many resemblances in our experiences that helped us look at situations in their upmost details on one hand and put into perspective that same situation by looking at it as part of a micro and macro environment. Daniela's life experience shaped her relationship with brands and

and her exposure to different brands, across different markets, throughout her career only contributed to expanding her horizons.

We are both "people persons", and we love retail because we have a chance to *be* in a particular location and to *exchange* with a particular *someone*. We both love retail because it is a dynamic environment, it is beautiful, personal and customizable. It embraces big and small; it values old and new. And for the love of retail, we believe that it is our duty to provide an eye opener about current brand practices and provide information about potential brand processes. But we know that we live in turbulent times and that the past few years have been challenging; from recession to pandemic, from a shift from physical to virtual to physical, the rise of social media and the development of social selling. . . . We believe that these turbulent times have only contributed to changing the face of retail; and we are here to provide retailer with a guide to survive and strive during these turbulent times.

On June 29th 2021, Daniela and I were having a quick lunch at the newly reopened department store in Paris.

While we were waiting for our salads to be served, Daniela asks "What are you looking for?". "An outlet or a plug to charge my phone", I answered. We both looked at each other and shook our heads.

- Isn't the retail experience about making the customer's life more convenient? A newly (re)opened department store or a simple store should at least provide the space for customers to charge their phones. We use our mobile phones so much that charging is a necessity!
- It is about the little things, I reply.
- Our mission is to shed the light over the uncomplicated and relevant retail practices that help brands provide better customer experiences.

Retail should be everything but complicated.

Retail should be nothing but customer-centric.

We invite you to take some time to accompany us through the pages of this book.

We have a thing or two to share with you!

Ghalia and Daniela

The fashion retail industry. How is today different from yesterday?

The fashion industry was shaken because many environmental factors have forced brands to rethink their "raison d'être" and their strategies. It was either a question of ethics related to fashion production and supply, to environmental aspects related to cotton harvest, dyeing or decoloring, fashion waste or greenwashing, or it was related to costs of maintaining fashion businesses and the perception of the fashion item. The fashion industry is looking at alternative ways to cater to its customers. Through and after the pandemic, many brands assisted in virtual fashion shows, and many have adopted live shopping or one-to-one digital selling. The physical retail spaces are being coupled up with online channels and customer experiences are becoming valuable assets to brands and customers.

This introductory chapter looks at developments and disturbances that marked the retail environment and the fashion industry during the past two decades.

The retail environment witnessed many happenings during the past two decades. This is seen at the social, cultural, economic, technological and ecological levels. The speed of development that occurred during the past 20 years was equal to all developments that occurred in the 200 years prior. Then the past couple of years' developments (or disturbances) have been said to have introduced as much as the past two decades. How about brands operating in these environments? What is their status today? How is the future looking to them? Do they even have a clear vision of the near future? They are being introduced to new retail operations, retail formats and retail functions. They are also questioning whether retail, as the world knew it, will keep finding its place in this turbulent environment.

Already existing retail brands could find themselves reassessing their situations and looking for new ways of developing or growing their businesses, to sustain and stay relevant to consumers. Entrepreneurial brands, wishing to enter the market, could be facing more uncertainties as they have no data that makes sense. This is problematic for their decision-making. Could this jeopardize all retail management knowledge? Would this grant brands sufficient knowledge to pursue their retail journey? When times are uncertain

DOI: 10.4324/9781003173212-1

and retail environments unpredictable, brand managers and entrepreneurs could develop instant decision-making reflexes. This could limit their assessment, visibility and their ability to evaluate. Instead of transcending over a given situation or looking around it, they tend to draw the shortest lines or take the fastest decisions before moving to the next steps. Is this managerial behavior sound? Is this temporary managerial impulsiveness guided by a brand's strategy or is it a momentary reaction to save a situation? Quoting Sun Tzu, who said that "Strategy without tactics is the slowest route to victory. Tactics without strategy is the noise before defeat". If we isolate this moment in time and evaluate brand managers' tactical decisions, could we say that they are going straight into a dead end?

This is all giving us a headache.

An overview of the fashion retail industry and the major actors, forces or happenings that are shaping it up

Less dullness, more excitement: an emotional currency

Already, in the 1980s, the need for a different take on marketing was due; it was a means of breaking out of a monotonous marketing and communications pattern. The term "Guerilla Marketing"[1] refers to "unconventional" tactics including elements of surprise. Undertaking an emotional customer approach is said to have a more valuable impression on customers in comparison to more "traditional" forms or marketing communications. Putting effort in extracting customer emotions was an advancement in marketing and advertising; it was also an acknowledgment that the customer is at the heart of retail.

Naturally, marketers and retailers reassess, reevaluate, lookout for trends and forecast directions in which their brands would be going. As part of a lively environment, businesses look out for "things or tools" to help them grow and evolve. Technology and technological advancements have had a major impact on retail brands. Again, there is nothing new in this; advancements in manufacturing pushed production and contributed to fast consumption. Physical retail formats accommodated all that production and were touchpoints for access to that offering. The internet contributed to retail advancements and shifted in consumption patterns.

Back in 1984, a "72-year-old woman, sitting down in her armchair at home, used her television remote control to place an order of margarine, cornflakes and eggs".[2] Back then, a "Videotext" technology generated a shopping list on an individual's television, then the order was phoned in to a local grocer. The goods were sent to the customer's home "like magic".[3] At this point, it was clear that consumers' shifting behaviors were at the heart of retail change. They embraced that change and democratized the way we consume. During the 1990s, consumption and access to consumption offerings could be done differently. The world was yet to whiteness, not only a retail channel or retail format's introduction, but a new reality: A customer does not have to necessarily go to a specific location to have access to information or products. Customers were "okay" with remote shopping and welcomed the idea of a digital sphere allowing them to have access to information, compare information or shop. Certainly, Amazon and eBay set the basis for online shopping, which we now know, and became leading entities dominating today's retail industry.

The 1990s was a decade of transformation: it evolved the concept of remote shopping by investing in online commerce. Driven by globalization, online commerce (e-commerce) became a viable channel. E-commerce started gaining its place in the retail environment and in consumers' shopping patterns and behaviors. However, by the end of the decade, retailers were confronted with a new reality that is not related to technology, e-commerce or retail formats; it was related to customers and their position vis-à-vis consumption. Given the array of product and services choice, the possibility to access the offering and information about it more easily, the multiplication of commercial centers, high streets and online stores, the offering seemed less interesting. The faster the changes happened, and options made available, the more customers got bored.

From extracting commodities to making goods, delivering services and finally staging experiences, the progression of Economic Value, as Pine & Gilmore[4] call it, highlights the importance of customization. Customers no longer value "things" or the "convenience of accessing" them, what they started looking for is the experience of accessing those things. Only those personal and memorable experiences mattered. At this point, brands delivering experiences were those engaging with customers in personal ways and doing that in places that are more staged, that are theatrical.

Yes, online retailing was growing and taking shape in the retail environment. And yes, physical retail was undergoing changes and it was in desperate need of dusting off its older self. If a product could magically arrive at the customer's doorsteps and if access to information could be done at the comfort of one's home, then what reason will a customer have to go to a store?

Mass, but personalized. Now that's something!

Imagine that a customer is admitted to a hospital to get treated. This customer (referred to as a patient in that case) would be admitted to a hospital that everyone else could have been admitted to, into a room that everyone else could have temporarily occupied and been assisted by nurses and doctors like everyone else would normally have. This patient, however, would not have received the same medication or treatment exactly as everyone else, simply because of the attention that everyone should be receiving, given his personal diagnosis. We could also imagine a customer going into a restaurant to have a steak. While the restaurant only serves meat, this customer would want a "well done" steak as opposed to another who is okay with "medium-rare".

The fashion retail industry paid much attention to customization as it was one of the tools helping in creating differentiation or a competitive advantage. Naturally, this process took some time to find its place within brand processes. Unlike tailor-making, which is a time-consuming and very costly process, customization allows customers to add on their personal touch to a product that the brand had already developed.[5]

Customization is a brand's strategic mechanism that requires careful alignment between its process and customer needs.[6] Since brands cannot predict what each customer would ask for, they should be able to offer customization options in a way that adds value to the existing business. How could a retail brand offer customization? To what extent would it customize and how much would it charge for that customization? When some brands picked up on the customization wave, the greater majority still did not. Most importantly, when looking at brand customization or personalization, the customer appears at the heart of the process. Empowered and considered as an integral part of the decision-making process, or acquisition process, customers knit stronger ties with the brands in question.

Brands had to rethink a physical store's environment, and later on, the virtual store's environment, in and through which the process of customization will take place. Now that the understanding of consumption has gone beyond the mere acquisition of products and services, retail will encompass, in addition to monetary transactions, an emotional exchange. Evidently, having chosen a color or pattern for a tennis shoe, or patching up a pair of jeans[7] makes the experience meaningful and the purchase more personal and relevant.

Is it the year 2000 already?

The foundation of online shopping dates to the 1980s and it was not until 1995 that online retailing took a better shape; transactional websites were thriving and secure e-commerce payment systems developing. In parallel with all marketing and communications actions that retailers traditionally adopted, it was possible to advertise a business, or brand, on the online sphere.[8] Shopping, pre-year 2000 and post-year 2000, has added up a new description to its initial definition. Initially defined as a browsing activity of the available goods and services presented by retailers, with an intent to purchase, the meaning of shopping has changed with e-commerce. The physical store was no longer the only point of contact where retailers and customers undergo exchanges and transactions.

The prevailing context shifted from a commercial and transactional focus to a social focus. Who is socially connected with whom? that thing called Facebook[9] mesmerized the world. Literally. Although younger users adhered first to the social network, many enthusiasts found themselves jumping on that train and taking part in this exciting journey. Geographical proximity was no longer an issue and individuals (or adherents) slowly integrated digital communications to their routines. As the access to information and information generation became easy, it opened the possibility to brands to take advantage of the platform and communicate, in turn, to adherents or potential customers.

We soon understood that the world has fewer reservations regarding many things and was more open to accepting that previous categorizations and labeling must be revised. Communications and consumption have begun their transformation process; a new era or "Ubiquitous Consumption"[10] begins to settle down:

> Internet and technology are no longer a "thing that young people use".
> Everyone likes to connect. It is a "human thing".
> Family, friends, love, birth, death . . . are "universal things".
> Sharing and receiving information are "now normal things".

With the addition of newer shopping formats on new shopping spheres, new retail strategies and shopping behaviors emerged. This meant that customers could search for information online, make their purchase online and receive their items at a desired address. As opposed to "going to" a store to look for, or purchase, an item, these products are now "coming over" to the customer's doorstep. A dissociation of marketing and retail took place. We could distinguish the physical store, the digital store, the physical storefront, the digital storefront, traditional brand and retail communications and digital brand and retail communications. Each element became and fundamental entity.

Online, offline, anytime, anywhere, right here or there

Customers had more possibilities to shop. For example, going window shopping for ideas and social recreation, then, as soon as they came back home, they could connect online, compare their preferred item across different retailers, decide on one product and one brand and finally, make the purchase. Once received, customers could consume products or return them back to the retailer. The beginnings of online shopping and the possibility of moving smoothly between online and offline were not as easy as it is today. It took quite some time for "newer" shopping to become seamless and frictionless; the beginnings were tough, yet promising. Then comes the smartphone,[11] and this time, not only as a mere technological device but as an indispensable extension of oneself. Using the internet was no longer restricted to a computer desk at home or the office. Customers became more mobile and had access to information faster, with convenience and almost anytime, anywhere. Their mobile phones became smarter and facilitated the process of access and exchange.

Online retailing slowly infiltrated consumers' shopping patterns. They grew to learn about different shopping possibilities. If a physical store had defined opening and operating hours, the online retail store was open 24/7. The online store also accelerated online payments and online payment securities. The online retail environment developed its own calendars; the "Cyber Monday" sale for instance. Moreover, shipping and delivery became a major competitive advantage to online retailers. With Amazon, not only fast deliveries were offered circa the year 2005, but the possibility to become a "prime" member and benefit from exclusive discounts and the possibility of a next-day delivery;[12] now that was something!

Online communities and the power of words

Blogging was also an important instance that coupled with many web-related advancements at the beginning of the century.[13] From a marketing and retail perspective, individuals grew to become content generators who mastered all topics that they talked about. More knowledge was curated, diffused online and made available to those who see the value in it. The source of influence was no longer dropped down from certified or trusted sources; individuals could also share content that others will judge as useful or valuable. The trend grew from technical blogging to lifestyle blogging and then to vlogging. Individuals, self-proclaimed experts, became more knowledgeable and looked-for sources as they were perceived as authentic and relatable.

Individuals become sources of influence that brands took to their advantage. Here again, comparing traditional media strategies to online media strategies, another approach with regards to whom represents the brand took place. Traditionally, brands communicated as per their guidelines. Brand identity elements had to be respected and applied to all communications formats. When choosing a figure, or persona, to represent a brand, it had to mirror its image and, always reflect its personality and standards. Choosing a celebrity to represent and/or endorse the brand was like a life-long marriage.

Now that many tools were at the disposal of individuals, they could self-curated content that is of interest to them. More importantly, they could get as creative as they can by doing so. Those individuals became themselves a brand and caught the attention of followers as well as retail brands. We are not talking about an international actor, boxer, fashion model or novelist. The next-door neighbor is the one whom millions follow for her cupcake recipes or her tips on well-being. A sophomore pupil has developed a new mobile application, and the teenager who was in love with her mother's old garments is now teaching the world how to recycle and re-use.

Retail brands are pretty much interested in "individual brands" as they have gained a considerable following. If this "following" could be relatable to the traditional concept of "market share", then yes, retail brands had to pay close attention and address individual brands more seriously. The question was not related to the choice of the person who will represent the retail brand, but the one who will best advocate, expand the reach and cultivate peers about it. A new form of retailing also developed with the growth of bloggers and influencers. They acted as intermediaries for established retail brands, promoted entrepreneurial ventures or even developed their own brands. These blogger/influencer-native brands stood in front of retail brands, armed with the power of their word, their looks and lifestyle but not their commercial offerings.

Production and mass production thrived during the industrial age; with the beginnings of this millennium, technology invaded the retail environment. With these new technologies came along new opportunities, new inventions and thoughts related to a new dimension of retail and consumption. A YouTube trailer description of an online game "Second Life" explained: "A new society, a new world created by you. Explore a world of surprise and adventure. Create anything you can imagine. Compete for fame, fortune or victory. Connect with new and exciting people". With such online games, individuals could re-imagine their persona in a second life and construct their life's narrative into that parallel dimension. As trivial as this sounded to many, the very few who adhered to this universe were looking for all essentials and non-essentials to be able to live and function in that new society. Retail brands also exploited this universe and saw the opportunity to be present, to take part of individuals' lives and their needs. They opened their virtual stores and gave individuals (residents) the possibility to dress with brand products. Some retail brands also provided a possibility to create custom versions of their products "for both their avatars and their real-world selves".[14]

With every opening, retail brands try to take advantage of the situation. Whether it was to increase equity, visibility or sales is not the main concern. What is important to underline is the desire to be present in any way possible, at any time possible and in any form possible. In the real world, retail brands grew from pure physical formats to online formats. As soon as the opportunity allowed them to conceive and develop a presence in a virtual dimension, they have done that, and they have done it by adapting their formats to meet that dimension's requirements.

No money? No biggies. You can rent it if you want it

Promoting fashion ownership was at the heart of the greater majority (if not all) brand marketing and communications strategies. A common managerial understanding was that of presenting items and either pushing or pulling them in a way that all activities would yield sales and returns. That business and management state of mind ruled for decades if not centuries. If on one hand retailers and retail brands lived by that management motto, customers, on the other hand, have been conditioned to act/react in a conforming manner.

But fashion came at "a cost" to customers as they had to allocate a considerable amount of their disposable income to maintain their wardrobes updated and up to date. And fashion was dominating consumers' lives; its ownership reflected their social status, standards and style. However, keeping up with an intense ownership and consumption trend started facing many complications. Be it related to the customer, the retailer, the fashion retail ecosystem or other *milieus* (economical, environmental, technological, political or legal).

Fashion rentals appeared as a solution; not welcomed with wide open arms, but very promising. Back in 2004, a fashion accessory rental website listed items that customers could rent for a period and for a percentage of the item's initial cost. After temporary consumption, items could be returned, otherwise kept and purchased. Some fashion critics hailed fashion rental describing it as a refreshingly guilt-free model,[15] a sustainable model or described it as an "infinite closet".[16] It took quite some time for this model to take root in the fashion retail industry; it may be since there was major desire to delay retail models that could replace direct production and sales.

Looking at fashion rental from a fashion business perspective is a great opportunity for brands. When deconstructing all steps that a fashion brand must go through before being fully operational is the conception, sampling, sourcing and manufacturing. This exorbitant and time-consuming process could be a liability, when and if, mismanaged. Fashion rental platforms "stock" with references that already exist, thus skipping all the tiresome parts. Another advantage is choosing references that the rental platform is going to exhibit. This choice could be conformed to prevailing fashion trends and consumption tendencies.

The retail environment is changing and so do customers

Another recession[17] hits and changes the way consumers consume. Back in 2008, the economy collapsed causing a major drop in retail sales and an alarming break in consumer consumption. In response to that, and to liquidate merchandise excess, retailers got into extreme markdown behavior. The offering became very accessible and low-priced, to the extent that customers were no longer willing to pay an extra dime to get what they want; they simply went elsewhere if they were not satisfied. A new wave of crisis-born customers became deal-sensitive or even "conditioned" to wait for better deals or markdowns?

Luxury brands, very concerned about the prevailing situation, have invested in an online presence to keep (and have) more control over their merchandise and prevent cheaper inventory from flooding the market in the case of other economic slumps.[18] Having taken a stand and been at the reserved side of e-commerce, luxury brands saw themselves entering the digital world alongside other lower-end brands. The post-recession retail environment's spectrum has stretched from luxury and hard discounts. Every "in-between" concept has found itself in an uncomfortable position: what should be done to draw customers into the store (online and offline) and make them want to spend?

The rise of e-commerce and access to information allowed customers to search for the best deals as opposed to searching for other quality or features. Equipped with their smartphones, they had the power to bargain if not the last word. More than ever, customers' attention turned to dollar stores and discount stores. Customers stopped showing up to the physical store if they did not see value in the effort that they were putting to get there. This depression also shifted mentalities; "why should I own" has earned a new connotation. Instead of thinking of reasons why one should purchase something, customers have begun to think of reasons why they should not purchase it. Thrift shopping, once categorized for the "weak-walleted",[19] was now considered a place of search and discoveries, a place where "gems" are found. More recently, rental and sharing found their natural place in customers' daily lives. The more "loyal" they are to the brand, the more they earn benefits, get discounts or receive products faster. Consumers became okay with sharing and wearing what does not initially belong to them.

It was very common to invest in physical retail locations and expand the business reach. It was agreed that building space and opening stores will only draw new customers in and help in growing sales. Retailers who have pushed for space acquisition, naturally required resources, operations and human resources. They found themselves in an embarrassing situation at the time of the recession: what should become of the stores? Which of the store should remain? What should be done with the stock excess? This situation was also a retail management wake-up call inviting brands to assess and evaluate before making their next move. Customers who have always met brands at their physical store and hailed all their offerings; this abruptly stopped seeing value in their store visits. The role of physical spaces and physical retail spaces was questioned. Is it a place of supply? Because the e-commerce sites are filling that function. Is it a place of product presentation? What's the big deal, then, to have as many places presenting the same offering?

Retail giants and department store closures became an everyday normal after the recession. Vacant stores, vanishing retailers, deserted high streets, low investments in retail . . . but there was a beacon of hope on the horizon: Pop-up stores and temporary retail. Agile, flexible and endowed with their ability to excite customers, these store formats appeared as a great solution for proprietors, retailers and customers. Pop-up stores have focused on variables that are very different from those previously exploited in traditional retail.[20] The physical pop-up store is a meeting space, a dynamic, bubbly and action-packed happening. It does not conform to traditional retail rules even if it borrows many aspects from it.

Pop-up stores became alternative retail formats through which brands, flaunt their creativity on one hand, and aim at meeting different communications, distribution and sales objectives on the other hand. These formats found their natural place in the retail environment. Even it took retailers some time to understand that pop-up stores are not here to replace traditional retail nor provide a solution to a suffering retail environment, they managed to get the best out of them and help ease struggling retail models.

Reviving lifeless retail

The talks about "suffering retail" have been around for quite some time; nothing new there. The recession did uncover the urgency of acting upon retail processes. These talks have been going for the decade, even two, preceding the recession. If retail experiences were the natural continuation proceeding transactional retail, why haven't retailers (re)invested in those? Going back to the age of H.G. Selfridge (founder of Selfridges, London) or A. Boucicaut (founder of Le Bon Marché Rive Gauche, Paris), retail was all about creating experiences. Their retail management methods succeeded in revealing the splendor of retail and mesmerizing consumers. A department store became a third place, a haven for those seeking refinement and style. It was also synonymous with innovation, novelty and creativity. But retail and commerce dried up during the industrialized age and, for the exception of very, it focused on being product-centricity.

Many brands invested in flagship stores to put forward their story, know-how and a lifestyle. They understood that they had to give customers something to aspire to, something to relate to and that is not necessarily a product. Other brands have looked at investing in concept places or third spaces. Customers enjoyed going out to do their shopping, have a cup of coffee and taste a cake all in one place. Flagship stores and concept stores took shopping to another dimension:[21] Loud music, fun staff, a wide selection of merchandise and inclusion of different services in-situ; stylist, personal shopper, hairdresser, nail art, personalization and so on.

Retail formats (especially those of fashion retail brands) have paid much attention to emotions. Investing in emotion-inducing spaces does not necessarily yield instant transactional return but strengthens the brand's equity. A flagship store, a physical store, a concession and an online store as well as other retail formats were necessary to maintain a brand's viability. It was time to reinject some life, some dynamic in retail. Investments in the retail atmosphere have proven the influence it could have on customer emotional and behavioral reactions. Manipulating atmospheric variables, such as sound, light or music, showed that they could affect an individual's time spent, choice of product and product purchase.

Reinforcing a retail store's social dimension was not to be neglected. It was more difficult to have a product-related competitive advantage, therefore, a shift toward the augmented offer took place. The mere act of purchase was no longer at the heart of shopping: the context in which the purchase is made became more valuable and spoke to consumers. The "human" dimension was re-invested. It was not a question of being served at a luxury fashion brand or on the high street, customer service and a non-invasive human presence were here to stay.

With the proliferation of in-store technologies, retail acquired another characteristic. Visiting a fashion retail store gave the possibility for an individual, not necessarily a customer, to discover the space and the offering and get in touch with the brand and with other peers. As there are no obligations regarding the choices of digitalized in-store hardware, each brand adopts that best suits them. Brands focusing on personalization, for example, invested in body scanners[22] and others in magic mirrors or fitting systems. There were also many brands that re-arranged their spaces to provide in-situ customization studios.[23] Online fashion brand websites and mobile applications also integrated interfaces facilitating customer choices and the purchasing process.[24]

A physical shopping experience became a social media sensation. Shopping with a friend, colleague or relative is a moment shared offline (in-store) and with their social community. QR codes, hashtags and weblinks, are highly present and visible in the physical retail store. It gave individuals the possibility to access and share information, compare products and delay the in-store purchase process to make it online or through other touchpoints. And yes, brand processes became smoother and customer processes safer and easier. Online payments and transactions are literally at the tip of customers' smartphones. Even though it took some time to figure a solution out, (fashion) retail channels managed to smoothen and soften all barriers by enhancing their stock accessibility and reading, facilitating stock deliveries and returns and integrating all payment facilities and securities.

Self-proclaimed connoisseurs, entrepreneurs, retailers and next-door neighbors

Brand, corporations, businesses and all those formal structures have tried to keep the situation "contained and controlled" for quite some time. They dictated the "what, how, where and whom" of fashion. For quite some time, individuals who did not conform to a trend or a "direction" were considered as the "black sheep" of their respective societies. Minorities where rather stigmatized, labeled and categorized. With the development of the internet a democratization took place. An individual could have his own website as legitimately as a brand could. Individuals became accustomed to seeing individual-sized websites and brand/organization-sized websites. Some developed very modest websites, others more developed, some very close to established brand standards and others less. If blogs allowed individuals to have their say about something, to teach, to give an opinion or to promote

With the advent of social media mobile applications and with the smartphone's capability to facilitate information input and output, personal communications and communications had taken on another meaning. An all-in-one piece that replaces a telephone, a camera, a laptop, a desk or even an external drive; the smartphone gave the possibility to self-express using pictures, videos and words and all this at the tips of one's hands. Whether projections are those of an individual or the individual's ideal self, all compilations of social media publications created a whole new universe: a new wave of thoughts, a rise of stylists, a rise of artists, a rise of home chefs, a wave of travel bloggers, personal fitness instructors, fashion and jewelry designers or business consultants.

Many individuals managed to grab the attention of others who shared an interest in what they had to show or say. With many "followings" (or followers), an average person became a person of influence. Followers wanted to go eat at the restaurant in which the influencer dined, they wanted to get that handbag and those pair of earrings that were worn during that dinner. Influencers started identifying brands[25] in their publications and gave them much visibility. A whole world of opportunities opened for individuals as at this moment, it was brands who paid much attention to whom will be the next influencer who will represent them.

Social media platforms introduced new features of paid advertising and added on many technical features enhancing user experience and community engagement. A mere text or photo became so "passé" and where soon replaced with videos and live sharing. The social media influencer wave became a business opportunity. For fashion retail, for example, it became a channel on its own right for presenting, promoting and selling fashion. At its infancy stages, influencers would tag a brand. Then there were paid partnerships[26] legitimizing the influencer/brand relationship. Social media platforms gave the possibility for an influencer and/or brand to link their accounts to a shop. A time saver and a direct link to the product; what else could a brand wish for?

Likewise, social media platforms and mobile applications highly promoted online marketplaces. Originally defined as a location in which a market is formed or held, an online marketplace does not have a different definition, just a different context. Another opportunity related to online marketplaces arises allowing individuals to regain their power over transactions without necessarily going through an "intermediate and formalized retail structure". Be it a handbag, a car, a house or a bicycle, the transaction and conditions are directly sorted by and between identified individuals.

Retail and consumption tensions. Are things always black and white?

The retail environment in general and the fashion retail environment have witnessed controverting developments in different areas and ways. To list a few:

Sustainable fashion and Polluting fashion
Fashion purchase and Fashion rental
Fast fashion and slow fashion
Mass fashion and luxury fashion
Firsthand fashion and second-hand fashion

If a fashion brand was at the stage of writing its marketing strategy 15 years ago, it would have gone through assessments related to internal and external environments affecting the brand on the short run and potentially affecting its growth. We assume that this brand had detected one of many external factors; an "environmental-related" factor such as that related to climate change. What would that have changed to the brand? To consumers? To retail environments? This little interrogation requires more than a book's chapter to resolve it; that we know. What we intend to direct the spotlight on is the fact that the prevailing retail environment is a reality, and it is what it is. Come to integrate change alone, brand actions will be insignificant. Whether there is the will, the mission or the power to maintain that change is one thing. The greater majority of brands, unfortunately, find themselves conforming (re-conforming) to the prevailing environment's realities to get a greater chance of survival.

Even if change happens and every market player recognizes it, they will not necessarily adopt it. Most consumers will eventually become more acquainted and acceptive of what brands may offer; will they directly consumer it? will they directly shift their consumption patterns? Are their actual behaviors going to mirror their intentions? From over-consumption to responsible consumption. From giant retailers to the next-door atelier, the fashion retail market was no longer dominated by giant dictator brands. Smaller brands resurfaced and catered to those who were looking for something different and new. Take for example customers purchasing from a next-door atelier that produces garments. Evaluating the item in question would be related to who made it, how much effort he put in making it and how it was made. This perception of value and worth gave hope to the fashion industry and to fashion consumption. The fashion retail's environment infrastructure and business models reflected a shift in consumer mindsets.[27]

What is sustainability? Is it just another trendy term that amuses fashion brands, retailers and the world? To date, it is difficult to sit on one single definition of sustainability; is the term related to planet earth, to climate change or to retail practices? It is better to refrain to "fashion sustainability"[28] as it frames the concept into processes related to the climate's integrity and all practices related to social justice. Even the definition has an altruistic meaning. Evolving around designing, sourcing and manufacturing fashion to maximize profit and minimizing the impact on the environment. A question of choices and ethics lie at the heart of sustainability. Climate crisis[29] flags have been raised and governments have started urging businesses to apply climate-reduction business models. The results, however, are still far from their original intentions.

Sustainability is also tightly connected to making different choices. Alternative textiles, alternative skins or even responsible textiles have been thriving. Fish skin, orange peel, pineapple, coffee grounds, corks, recycled rubber or mushrooms[30] are now alternatives to animal skin that were exploited in the fashion industry for so long. Natural dye is going hand-in-hand with the process of exploiting alternative textiles. As in any case, exploiting these areas started slowly and gained considerable attention from more established brands and consumers. Ditching fur and animal skin[31] was once an exception and is now a fashion fundamental principle. Looking at these practices also sheds the light on waste management and the utilities of natural waste in many ways. It also prevents many hazards that are related to tanning and chemical needed for the process of animal skin dying.

Sustainable practices that have been welcomed by customers and developed by brands were those related to circular fashion and the circular fashion economy. Yes, of course, there are fewer fashion manufacturing processes, but there is a lot to do with regards to distributions and deliveries; and this raised another concern of whether a fix-up somewhere is leading to a problem elsewhere.

A lot has changed in the retail environment during the past decade. These upheavals will be responsible for shifting retail and consumer practices. At a luxury brand level, used luxury blossomed online and with the development of many digital selling platforms.[32] These platforms were all about presenting a classic, a vintage, an iconic model and all about authentication. As this online luxury second-hand market grew and its audience grew, it expanded into physical retail through consignments.[33] Luxury brands' attention shifted to second-hand items and are now doing their bests to regain control over that market and their products. Fast-fashion brands also included these practices within the brand and retail strategies. It is becoming common to find a used or second-hand corners in a fast-fashion store. Each manifests the presentation and "treatment" of these references differently; some allow swapping, others sell them by the kilo,[34] and others have integrated them into their stock. Customers are more aware and more accepting of second-hand.

If they have been slowly processing a different mode of consumption, the pandemic and latest climate-related events have greatly contributed to the instauration of this concept in their minds and into their habits.

It was about time to do the math

A non-retail variable majorly influencing the retail environment circa 2019, and causing a state of chaos, took the world by storm. The impact of something that cannot be seen, nor controlled, was a total frustration and caused a global state of panic that was labeled Covid-19. It inhibited the world's capacity of acting or finding adequate solutions; yes because the world had grown on projecting based on prior givens and on taking actions based on assumptions. Well, with a new reality forcing itself upon the world, and with no room for anticipation it was time to take "re-act".

During the past two decades, digital commerce had settled along with physical commerce in the retail world. If physical and online retail were machines, they would have needed not only an environment to settle in, but a whole system allowing healthy operations and elements driving it. In a retail environment's setting, fueling retail channels operations needs many resources such as (and not limited to) human capital to produce, to communicate, distribute and to sell.

It certainly needs spending customers; individuals with the ability to repeatedly inject resources income at offline and/or online distribution channels. When the world went into lockdown mode, the machine's dynamic was disturbed.

As individuals were not authorized to go out or "going to" a physical store to fulfill their needs, they turned to online retail. During a short period of time, online retail sales rocketed, not because physical retail was less performant, but simply because it could not operate. To remedy human absence in physical stores, brands and retailers exploited all possible solutions to keep in touch, stay connected and attend to their customers. Social media platforms and mobile applications accompanied individuals and retailers, shortened the distance between them and lifted the isolation which they both commanded to. Luxury shopping experiences majorly taking part in sumptuous set-ups, were happening remotely. Luxury personnel had to re-adapt to the digital context and keep the brand standards intact. Middle-range brands, mass brands, entrepreneurial and artisanal brands all had to rethink their existing models to stay alive, in consumers' minds and hearts.

Everything that used to happen "physically" was revised to reencourage customers' return to stores in a sanitary atmosphere. New retail rules were put in place: customers were required to wear a mask, have their smartphone ready with a vaccination QR code, apply hand sanitizer at the store's entrance and disinfect the supermarket shopping cart; a wider use of contactless payment was put in place. Systems for keeping a physical distance when queuing up and controlling the number of customers per square meter were established, with enter only, exit only and circulation indications, plus more click & collect and home deliveries.[35] With retail being "hands-on", it became "hands-off"[36] and touch-free.

Individuals and brands got together online and on social media. Live concerts, live product presentations, live chats, live shopping[37] or augmented reality for easier product trials became common. It was not a question of marketing practice, it was simply a reality that everyone had to adopt and adapt to. Smaller brands and entrepreneurs didn't hesitate to have their own voices heard during the pandemic. Showing what's in store took a very natural orientation and consisted of real-time commentaries and storytelling. Many rules and norms of retail were set aside to welcome more authentic and uncomplicated ways of communications and sales. As digital (momentarily) took over, and customers were no longer going out, the consumption of many "things" related to commuting, travel, office and shopping for non-essentials dropped.

Many fashion brands looked at non-physical fashion, other brands concentrated of offerings that are home related, home wear collections or well-being and health products and services. Shopping malls and department stores suffered as they could not open their doors and physically welcome consumers. Many have looked at solutions to arrange virtual store visits or to connect interested customers with a sales representative or a team member to help them do their shopping. Boundaries blurred during the pandemic and with digital technologies contributed to a "boundaryless retail environment". Online, offline, through the line, experiential, ephemeral, digital . . . whatever it is, whatever it was called, the physical and digital world never found themselves closer and more integrated in individual lives.

After having been put to the test, retailer and retail brands took down the customer-centric road. A retail brand's existence was to serve the customer, provide him with a solution, facilitate his journey and his experience. Retail brands had to be present, conversational, engaging, reactive and authentic. A re-evaluation of all brand/customer touchpoints recently developed in the sense that, some or all brand distribution and communication channel usage and utilities could have been allocated a different purpose.

The "physicality" of retail moved away from rooting in one specific place. A brand's "physical store" could come over to the customer, come closer to his neighborhood and home.[38] Now, the form that this physical store takes could be anything. This is not restricted to integrating pop-up store events into the brand's strategy, it could be a regular and repeated action conforming to the customer's schedules and needs. More pick-up lockers were installed or dispatched for facilitate order picks ups: restaurants, supermarkets or fashion retailers.[39]

Subsequently, retail had become more ambulant,[40] rotary and adaptive.[41] On one hand, retailers move from their respective areas to discover others and to get in touch with potential customers or facilitate the exchange with their clients. On the other hand, unoccupied Highstreet spaces on the highstreets or other retail conglomerates, are being hired not only for shorter periods of time but for fractions of periods. Micro-leasing a boutique or any space for half a day or just a couple of hours is becoming more common and more practiced in the retail world.

Today's retail is all about the unification of commerce. It makes no sense at all to divide and devise a brand into departments and components. Brands should be holistically managed to deliver a holistic customer engagement and experiences. Searching online, purchasing during a social media live session, receiving at home and returning in store is only normal and have become the norm. Despite the bodily differentiation between physical and digital, today's retailers and retail brands are looking at all possibilities keeping seamless transitions in and between those universes. A physical store opens a portal to the digital store or bridges to a parallel dimension. The metaverse is not here and present more than ever; if there was suspicion on all retail-related discussions and conflicts that have been made during the past decades, there will be no doubt that a fundamental change is has already started.

What's in it for fashion retail brands?

"In the midst of every crisis, lies great opportunity", Einstein says. Fashion retailers and fashion retail brands are already looking at many opportunities amidst prevailing chaos. The retail environment is still made of brands, organizations, suppliers, distributors, competitors and customers. what's changing is the nature of their relationship, dependency and relevancy: Does a (fashion) brand need a supplier and a retailer and is their relationship going to be identified as vertical or horizontal? Is a (fashion) brand's survival going to be solely depending on the supplier's performance? Will the (fashion) brand's offering be relevant to customers? or is the way the offering is presented, or made accessible, relevant to customers?

Could it be possible that human needs have changed? and will referring to Maslow's hierarchy[42] of needs accurate? Is presenting the brand's offering according to the marketing Ps, Cs, Es and Vs still relevant? At the heart of marketing is benchmarking, assessing, evaluating and predicting. However, with everything changing and causing disturbance, there are no safe grounds to set foot on, yet alone have visibility. As the retail environment gets foggy, retailers are shortsighted and less equipped with certainty.

This is not promoting negativity in retail, only shedding a light on a situation that seems less familiar than the one that brands and retailers were long accustomed to. One thing is certain though: Commerce and retail are part of the human fabric. They have existed before even being studied a marketing function. Today, we dare to say that marketing and retail . . .

Evolved.

Changed form.

But at the essence, it is very true to its ethos, very much linked to value and still rooted within the human and the human experience. Managing fashion retail brands and retail in general is in desperate need of renew; their problems cannot be solved using the same thinking that was used when they were created (Einstein, A). In the following chapters, we will be sharing our thoughts, suggestions and vision on how to manage fashion brands in a turbulent retail environment.

Notes

1. Guerilla marketing: www.creativeguerrillamarketing.com/what-is-guerrilla-marketing/
2. Lufkin, 2020. Available at: www.bbc.com/worklife/article/20200722-the-curious-origins-of-online-shopping
3. Miva, 2016. Available at: https://blog.miva.com/the-history-of-ecommerce-how-did-it-all-begin
4. Pine & Gilmore, 1998. *Welcome to the Experience Economy*. Boston: Harvard Business School Press; Pine & Gilmore, 1999. *The Experience Economy: Work is Theatre & Every Business a Stage*. Boston: Harvard Business School Press
5. Zhang, 2021. Mass customization: The new path for luxury industry? Available at: https://hapticmedia.com/blog/mass-customization-definition-goal-examples/
6. Salvador, Martin de Holan & Piller, 2009. *Cracking the Code of Mass Customization*. MIT Sloan. Available at: https://sloanreview.mit.edu/article/cracking-the-code-of-mass-customization/#article-authors
7. The Levi's® Tailor Shop Offers Up Customizations of its Iconic Back Patch. Available at: https://hypebeast.com/2019/8/levis-tailorshop-agr-knit-alicia-robinson-custom
8. Ang, 2021. Key events in the history of online shopping. Available at: www.visual capitalist.com/history-of-online-shopping/
9. Hall, 2021. Facebook. Available at: www.britannica.com/topic/Facebook
10. Cox, 2004. Ubiquitous consumption and the marketing mix, *Journal of Internet Commerce*, 3:2, 21–32, DOI: 10.1300/J179v03n02_02
11. Tocci, 2019. History and evolution of smart phones. Available at: https://simplexting.com/where-have-we-come-since-the-first-smartphone/
12. Ang, 2021. Key events in the history of online shopping. Available at: www.visual capitalist.com/history-of-online-shopping/
13. Themeisle, 2021. The history of blogging: From 1997 until now. Available at: https://themeisle.com/blog/history-of-blogging/
14. Kuntze et al., 2013. The rise and fall of virtual reality retailing in second life: An avatar's perspective, *Journal of Management and Marketing Research*
15. Conlon, 2020. The rise of fashion rental. Available at: www.theguardian.com/fashion/2020/sep/20/the-rise-of-fashion-rental-scarlett-conlon
16. Lieber, 2020. The fashion rental market tested and explained: Who has the best service? Available at: www.businessoffashion.com/articles/technology/fashion-rental-market-rent-the-runway-nuuly-le-tote-vince-unfold/
17. Andres, 2018. Divided decade: How the financial crisis changed retail. Available at: www.marketplace.org/2018/12/20/what-we-learned-retail/
18. Thomas & Hirsch, 2018. 10 years after the financial crisis, Americans are still looking for a deal. Available at: www.cnbc.com/2018/09/18/ten-years-after-the-financial-crisis-were-still-looking-for-a-deal.html

19. Martinez, 2017. What's the difference between thrift stores and vintage shops? Available at: Https://studybreaks.com/culture/vintage-shops/
20. Jenkin, 2015. Are pop-up shops high street heroes—or just a temporary fix? Available at: www.theguardian.com/small-business-network/2015/nov/05/pop-up-shops-high-street-heroes
21. An example of the former TopShop, Abercrombie & Fitch®, Citadium, the former Colette and so on
22. Peters, 2020. This body scanner creates custom jeans that fit you perfectly. Available at: www.fastcompany.com/90569484/this-body-scanner-creates-makes-custom-jeans-that-fit-you-perfectly
23. For example, the Nike ID studio or L'atelier du soulier at Le Bon Marché. Lerévérend, 2017. Le Bon Marché fait le pari de la personnalisation et du sur-mesure. Available at: https://fr.fashionnetwork.com/news/le-bon-marche-fait-le-pari-de-la-personnalisation-et-du-sur-mesure,821781.html
24. For example, Pepe Jeans, Levi's, Dior, Goyard and so on
25. Wagner, 2019. The power of social media influencers: Why it works. Available at: https://stevens-tate.com/articles/the-power-of-social-media-influencers-why-it-works/
26. Find Your Influence, 2021. A history of social media influencers. Available at: https://findyourinfluence.com/a-history-of-social-media-influencers/
27. Cernansky, 2022. Sustainability: Where fashion is heading in 2022. Available at: https://www-voguebusiness-com.cdn.ampproject.org/c/s/www.voguebusiness.com/sustainability/sustainability-where-fashion-is-heading-in-2022/amp
28. Inspired from Sustainable Jungle. Available at: www.sustainablejungle.com/sustainable-living/ethical-sustainable-fashion/
29. HechoxNosotros, 2020. The history of sustainable fashion. Available at: www.hechoxnosotros.org/post/the-history-of-sustainable-fashion?gclid=Cj0KCQiA2NaNBhDvARIsAEw55hivqA6En9TVeOcjGD6_EepKzqwYljRMAeF2QcvxiTDyXI-izEJAe54aAjdOEALw_wcB
30. Wolfe, 2020. Leaves, mushrooms, bark and more: 8 Innovative eco-friendly leather alternatives. Available at: https://goodonyou.eco/eco-friendly-leather-alternatives/
31. Hahn, 2020. Six alternatives to animal leather made from plants and food waste. Available at: www.dezeen.com/2020/10/16/leather-alternatives-vegan-materials-design/
32. Such as Vestiaire Collective, The Real Real, FashionPhile and others. Diwak, 2021. The rise of pre-owned luxury fashion marks a shift amid sustainability movement. Available at: https://retail-insider.com/retail-insider/2020/03/the-rise-of-pre-owned-luxury-fashion-marks-shift-amid-sustainability-movement/
33. Gleyse, 2020. This Parisian department store is the newest place to hunt for luxury vintage treasures. Available at: www.vogue.fr/jewelry/article/bon-marche-rive-gauche-collector-square-vintage
34. Desandes, 2021. En magasin, Pimkie s'ouvre à la vente de vêtements d'occasion au kilo. Available at: https://fr.fashionnetwork.com/news/En-magasin-pimkie-s-ouvre-a-la-vente-de-vetements-d-occasion-au-kilo,1299840.html
35. Vader, 2020. *The Realities of Retailing in a COVID-19 World*. KPMG. Available at: https://home.kpmg/xx/en/home/insights/2020/03/realities-of-retailing-in-covid-19-world.html
36. Repko & Thomas, 2020. 6 ways the coronavirus pandemic has forever altered the retail landscape. Available at: www.cnbc.com/2020/09/29/how-coronavirus-pandemic-forever-altered-retail.html
37. Coulet, 2020. Live shopping: la prochaine révolution retail. Available at: www.journaldunet.com/ebusiness/crm-marketing/1494509-live-shopping-la-prochaine-revolution-retail/
38. Yotka, 2020. What if the Louis Vuitton store came to you? Available at: www.vogue.com/article/louis-vuitton-mobile-store

39. An example of KFC restaurant and Tesco's self-service and click and collect lockers. Available at: www.verdictfoodservice.com/news/kfc-quick-pick-up/, and www.tesco.com/groceries/en-GB/zone/click-and-collect-lockers
40. Mortice, 2020. À Boston, le concept de commerce ambulant transforme le secteur de la vente. Available at: https://redshift.autodesk.fr/commerce-ambulant/
41. For instance, the services presented by Sook Space. Available at: www.sook.space/
42. For reference: https://www.simplypsychology.org/maslow.html

Chapter 1

How can fashion brands stay true to themselves?

Fashion brand conception, development and management have been following industry-set guidelines for many years now. Shared knowledge regarding what to do/not to do, how to, what to and when to guided brand managers with all aspects of their brand decision-making. Managing a fashion brand had to follow conventional guidelines, assessing its performance, evaluating and revising its decision-making processes whenever needed. Fashion brands had to decide where they want to compete on the market by choosing their place on the mass/luxury spectrum. Their identities were then developed accordingly, and they were set to take their first steps on the market. To what extent is this still relevant today? How can a brand stay true to its identity and face all "temptations" from other surrounding brands and their practices? Also, how can it follow management processes that are becoming less relevant to today's retail environment?

This chapter looks at fashion branding and marketing, however, the aim is not to rationalize this knowledge, rather to interpret it in ways that makes it clearer for the reader, how concepts are related to one another and how they affect one another in today's turbulent retail environment. For instance, it is not introducing the concept of branding, but to explain how branding affects the brand's positioning that in turn affects the brand's competitive position and so on. The fashion retail market is becoming more complex and competitive. Moreover, many concepts are being constantly introduced; some "wow" customers, some influence customer consumption patterns, others change customer habits or introduce new ones. Less established or less experienced brands can be tempted by some aspects of businesses that have gained important customer attention. Without a clear guidance or strategy, brands could risk deviating from their brands' ethos which might lead to the brand's failure. Lost between taking smaller and surer decisions or between taking instant and riskier actions, brands could find themselves in and out of business before they know it.

DOI: 10.4324/9781003173212-2

Holistic fashion brand management

A brand is first and foremost a social being that occupies a place in society and contributes, in a way or another, to its well-being. In a fashion retail context, the brand could engage in different sectors at different industry levels. With that guiding principle in mind, a brand occupies an integral place in society and in an environment. It is affected by, and affects, other brands and other individuals.

If brands resembled human beings, then. . . .

When one gives birth to a brand, conceives it, they know what the brand is at this moment in time, and would imagine what it would be some time after. The infant-brand will be taken care of, catered to and raised with love and affection. There could be extreme attachment and intensive feelings related to the brand; afraid to let go, or to look at the broader picture in which the brand-conceiver and infant-brand exist, decision-making might be less suited to the infant and lean more toward the conceiver; which is only normal and natural.

All through infancy and childhood, the brand's conceiver governs the brand by teaching it everything it knows and delivering as much information as possible to guide and accompany it in the environmental immersion period. During this period, the infant-brand will grow into a child-brand; its personality will be shaped. Every information that it has been given will affect its character, its preferences, its orientations and consequently, its choices. The child-brand will also learn how to look out for itself or choose those whom it feels more comfortable with. Others would have already spotted it and understood its potential; they would have wanted to befriend it or beware of it.

Embedded in a culture and starting to grow on its philosophy, the child-brand's energy develops and grows. The environment in which it's growing is nurturing and inspiring. It might look like a promising ground most of the times, threatening at other times. Every moment, every incident, every encounter is a lesson and a moment of reflection that helps the child-brand grow into an enhanced version.

The passage between childhood and maturity is no easy one as the brand faces many confrontations and could be very much drawn toward many temptations. Questions related to the "raison d'être", to what it's doing, it's offering, how it's adding value and what should be done next, all become part of the daily moments. The brand's conceiver has less control over what it has to say to the brand; it did its initial job and accompanied the infant into childhood. Now, its role is to serve the brand, through the choices it has made, into its adulthood.

Having become more sensible to the environment and its actors, the adult brand undergoes many improvement phases; the focus narrows to being clear on its identity, how others perceive it, what it does, how it does it and why it is better than anyone else at doing this. Having become more mature and confident, the brand presents and represents itself in a way that clearly defines its identity. The brand continues surrounding itself with those, very much like it, who share its vision, philosophy and feel connected to its culture. It seeks to grow its network within the direct environment and expand its business within the retail environment.

The brand becomes the "talk of the town"; respected by many, feared by some and certainly looked-up to by others, the mature brand feels like enjoying his moment of glory. Not fooled by the retail environment's calmness, the mature brand keeps its eyes and ears open more than ever. It stays put and alert as any mistake would be fatal at this point. How to keep the brand relevant? How to keep it desirable? How to stay ahead of the competition? it has earned its place in society, in its environment. Like any other member of this society, the brand's role will become more meaningful as it will be actively contributing, offering a service, delivering an exciting offering, presenting solutions, interlacing meaningful relationships or sharing experiences. As any member of society, the brand will find its balance, thrive, have its moment of glory, face difficulties or be less significant or less active.

With the great advances in artificial intelligence and the increasingly important contribution to society, would the idea of a non-human creating a brand[1] be far from reality? Would a brand's existence in a retail environment be anywhere different than any other active member of the society occupying that environment?

A Fashion Brand's Lifecycle Stages

Newborn * Child * Teenager * Active member of the fashion retail society

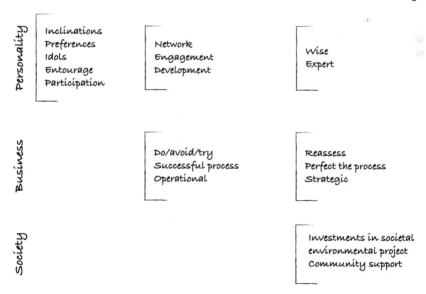

Figure 1.1 A fashion brand's lifecycle stages

Why yesterday's brands are no longer relevant in today's retail environment?

A holistic marketing orientation led many brands to focus on methods creating more value. This practice paid much attention to exploiting value, creating it and delivering it to build long-term relationships that are mutually satisfying to both, the brand and customer. Given the nature of the environment and its constituents, value creation was the result of a process involving many actors. This "dynamic environment" is made up of many actors who constantly look at ways to anticipate or meet customer needs better than the competition.

At first, a brand identifies a segment that it finds profitable and targets consumers that are more likely to react to its offering. Establishing a relationship between the brand and the target audience required a lot of attention to the brand's identity, its strategic direction and orientations. The brand then caters its offering to meet consumer's needs and wants, even, anticipate fulfilling their desires. Endowed with a concise identity, the brand would be seeking to identify only those customer segments who present great business opportunities.

With a clear positioning in mind, the brand shaped its offering to attend to customer expectations and deliver value throughout the process. Moreover, it aimed at projecting a congruent image that its targeted customers will perceive and integrate within their mindsets. In this brand management culture, the brands kept "fighting" to conquer and occupy the greatest mental space as well as the greatest market share. In a highly competitive market and a cluttered retail environment, standing out, highlighting a competitive advantage or even having a moment under the spotlight became a constant struggle. In a highly competitive retail environment, every brand aims for that larger piece of the cake; very few, however, could manage to have it.

The amalgamation of marketing and communications channels also became a new normal. Each brand's channel, whether distribution or communications, was managed to deliver value to customers and to facilitate the access to the brand's offering, or to get them in touch with the brand. Delivering a seamless and omnichannel experience became a major brand driver.

The digital revolution created an information age that promised to lead to more accurate production levels, more targeted communications, and more relevant pricing. It grew and evolved in a way that it managed to incorporate physical channels and leading to an era where physical and digital continuously flirt. Moreover, technological advances in transportation, shipping, and communication have enabled companies to market their products in almost every country in the world and consumers to buy from those countries. But then, a decade after the "great recession", there was a pandemic.

Despite moving away from a product-orientation and shifting toward value creation, a brand's existence in a retail environment was restricted to specific functions. The world was accustomed to the transactional nature of their relationships with most brands and more specifically fashion brands. In fact, fashion brands have been conceived and managed to "provide something" for customers in exchange of a monetary amount.

A new viewpoint on the (fashion) retail environment

The retail environment and its actors have been exposed to many changes during the past two decades. These challenges have been stimulating to some brands, sedating to others. They have contributed to, shifting processes and understandings, that have long been adopted by retail actors. These changes have greatly affected customers and consumption patterns; moreover, they contributed to changing the role and relationship dynamics between individuals, customers and brands.

A complex retail environment

Reading a retail environment and understanding how it works is now more challenging, and this is because the very fabric of this environment has been undergoing many modifications, the retail environments' dimensionality, the duality of its actor functions and the complexification of relationship identification between these actors. At the heart of this reading and observations, lies the (fashion) brand. As opposed to fashion brand management styles that have been long-adopted, current readings shed the light on new environmental realities that are not fundamentally changing "the brand", but its changing roles and functions.

The external retail and the direct retail environments have become more complex than ever. A clear designation of the nature of each environment must be made to reflect these new realities: a "physical or virtual external environment" and a "physical or virtual retail environment". Each environmental dimension has now established its own rules and operating guidelines that (fashion) brands must digest. Even though each dimension is integral, it cannot be the only one that the brand will be operating in. A physical brand will need a virtual representation, a virtual brand will need a physical representation, different types of brands will be looking at alternative retail environments that are relevant to them. Therefore, (fashion) brands are invited to understand each dimension's requirements and what they should be doing to stay relevant, or become operational, in each. However, given the realities that the world has come across, a brand would have less chances of survival if it doesn't open to connecting physical, digital and alternative dimensions.

Table 1.1 Alternative retail environments

	Physical	Phygital	Virtual	Alternative
Retail environment	Offline retail formats Physical offering Physical access to the offering Physical experiences Human interactions with the brands (and others)	A connector, a link, facilitating the transition between physical and virtual (or alternative) retail environments	Online retail formats (virtual stores) E-commerce (transactional websites) Virtual window sites Social media platforms Human interactions with the brand and others	Access through alternative realities A human representation with a brand representation and with other human representations
External environment	Production process Distribution process Raw materials Alternative raw materials (and others)		Technological advances Production process Delivery process Connectivity (speed) New currencies and exchange processes Access, ownership and securities	

The (fashion) retail environment's actors and their relationships are being questioned. In fact, their respective roles are evolving, to go hand-in-hand with all the developments and transforming: a duality of functions is more than ever present and prompting a change of dynamics (this book only highlights the main actors and explain how their roles and relationships are transforming).

Endowed with human characteristics, the brand becomes a social actor of its (fashion) milieu; the retail environment in which it acts. It will continually exercise its duties and claim their rights in society; like any other community member, it will be seeking ways to thrive, evolve, develop, live in a healthy environment that it shares with others. In the fashion retail environment's context, the "others" are all members of the society with whom the brand is in contact with, either directly or remotely.

Individuals have long been raised and accustomed to certain expectations from fashion retail brands. More recently, they have been questioning fashion brand behaviors or other issues related to fashion and fashion consumption. They also have become key players in the brand's formula as they are co-creating alongside the brand, conversing and exchanging with it. The times when customers had brands supplying them with valuable recourses is over now; brands are turning to "individual customers" or "individual brand customers" for alternative resorts. Many environmental developments have contributed to enhancing the retail environment in general, the retail format and retail brand more particularly. "Individual customer's" shopping experiences or overall journeys were enhanced and became closer to their daily routines. So, shopping and the access to the offering integrated the very fabric of an individual's lifestyle and his daily activities.

On her way to work, the customer goes into the next-door store, selects items she needs, pays for them and askes for the goods to be delivered at her door later in the evening. She takes public transportation and checks her social media sites for fun. She falls in love with a purse and wants to know more about its specifications; as soon as she clicks on the picture, she is redirected to the brand's online store. Knowing that the items could be returned for free, she places an order online and selects a nearby click-and collect store from which she will be picking the item from as soon as she received it. Going back to her social media page, she clicks on a live selling session. An influencer, that she has been following for quite some time now, is talking about her daily beauty routine and presenting different beauty care products.

Toward the end of the live session, the influencer shares a discount code with her audience; it would be a great opportunity to purchase the range of beauty care products with that discount code. The customer was intrigued enough to do it. Later, throughout the day and during her break, she logs on the beauty care website and check the collection that the influencer promoted during her live. She decides to go to the store that happens to be close to the office to check out and test the collection before she buys it using the discount code. Once in store, she tests the product and takes pictures of herself doing so. She tags the influencer and the brand as well as some of her friends. She doesn't purchase the items though; but it was a pleasurable experience.

The "individual customer" had not only been influenced by a brand; other actors, such as "individual customer brands" have become references in the retail environments. Call them agents or intermediaries, call them promoters, these individuals have become active brands. They don't qualify for the same status of a brand (or android brand), but they have the power to translate their actions into business. "Individual customer brands" took advantage of all facilities that online technologies have provided and took advantage of social media platforms. Any skill or passion they had was translated into a business-like form; for many, it turned into a proper business. Most importantly, these "individual customer brands" had something that brands saw as valuable; they had access to an audience. They didn't only have access to the audience, but they had the power to influence, advise, teach, accompany or even directly exchange with it. From a brand's perspective, "individual customer brands" have become an intermediary if not an access point to come closer to potential audience (or target audiences).

Brand, "individual customer", or "individual customer brand"; every actor plays now more that their indented role. An illustrator, for instance, working in an advertising agency could launch a T-shirt business selling a wide variety of t-shirts with his signature illustrations printed on them. Many "do-it-yourself" websites facilitate the task of the illustrator to launch a functional transactional website. Illustrator by day, illustrated T-shirt brand owner by night, a services supplier is also a fashion retailer. A customer's role has also evolved in the fashion retail environment. Some "individual customers" have kept their relationship restricted to the transactional form. Other "individual customer" brands have invested in a retail function; with a skill set that they have, or have acquired, they went into a business side of fashion.

"Individual customer brands" took advantage of many platforms that give them the opportunity to re-sell used garments and accessories. Another example is regarding those who have ventured into selling fashion; yes, but not designing or producing it. Instead by selecting available items and communicating them on their sites or social media pages. The transaction takes place through a simple website, a one-page or funnel website: the acclaimed "individual customer brand" places an order from the supplier who will make the item ready and ship it to the customer, who will receive it within the previously mentioned deadline.

If a customer was considered as valuable to the brand and considered as a valuable source of profit, it is now flagged as a potential competitor. Any "individual customer" could become an "individual customer brand" and by that become the brand's direct competitor. The (fashion) retail environment is no longer reserved for the elite or for very few; it has become the playground of many. Very few, however, will manage to stand out. A brand's offering is becoming less relevant in this context and if a (fashion) brand (and android brand) has not already integrated other factors to enrich their concepts, they would risk stepping down.

The fashion retail environment's actors are interchangeably affecting one another. The android brand influences the "individual customer" and the "individual customer brand". The "individual customer brand" influences the "individual customer" and the brand. Brand direct and indirect competitors could overshadow the brand, they also affect "individual customers" and "individual customer brands". In that retail environment, the android brand's role has evolved into being a social actor; it could speak and take actions like any other "individual customer". Customer roles have changed; they evolved into becoming active business entities and could be considered as brand competitors.

There is not only one entry to the fashion retail business. Anyone, any actor, can grow into becoming a brand. This being said, the (fashion) brand, competing brand(s) and "individual customer brands" operate alongside a variety of players that constitute the environment. If these were referred to as stakeholders, they would qualify to be also called actors in today's environment. These actor roles have also transformed: a service provider, a manufacturer, a distributer or any other business could be supplying to brands as well as developing their own. Many manufacturers have invested to develop their own retail distribution points. They would vertically integrate and have an advantage over other brands that have less control over their channel members. To be succinct, any player or actor has the power to develop their own brands. Not only this is overly complicating the (fashion) retail environment, but it also calls into question the supply concept. Supply chain or better call it a "convenience chain"? since all the actors are operating in the retail environment and managing to survive, then why a supply chain channel is even needed? Vertical, horizontal or whatever shape it takes, today's "convenience chain" is hyper-personalized and puts together all elements that the brand needs to survive and stay relevant.

Understanding a (fashion) brand in today's complex retail environment

In a turbulent retail environment, the majority of (fashion) retail actor roles have become more complex; the duality of roles demonstrates the ability of customers to adopt brand functions, and of brands to adopt "individual customer" behaviors. Given their integration and implication in the environment, fashion brands are now active members of their society. Like any

Retail environments' actors interchanging roles

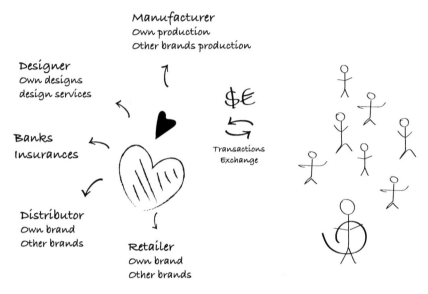

Figure 1.2 The retail environment's actors interchanging roles

other aspect of society, a (fashion) brand will practice its skills, perfect its business, reflect on its ideas, speak up its mind or display its set of interests.

Today's fashion retail brand is an active member of the fashion retail society

Not only the brand is described with human-like adjectives, but it has also become a human-like member, and an active member, of the fashion retail society. The fashion brand's society relates to the close circle in which it acts and with whom it constructs its journey. The role of that brand is not solely related to value creation and delivery through its offering; it could have other skills that it might like to share, it might be interested in other brands or "individual customer brand" skills or it could want to develop a new set of skills or other types of businesses at a certain point of its journey.

At its very essence,[2] the brand's "raison d'être" is the very constituent of its DNA. Questions like "why am I here" and "what I am going to do" are important instances in the brand's life as they will be guiding its choices and decisions. The question of "how am I going to be doing things" is crucial at this stage; attempting to answer this question will allow the brand to take a moment and think of the best ways of meeting its objectives, without damaging its society or environment. At a brand level, its upbringing and the way it was raised will greatly affect the actions and decisions that will be made. At the level of competition, will refusing an opportunity be considered a weakness? s mismanagement? As a leadership error? At a, "individual customer" and "individual customer brand" level, will the brand's altruistic decision have a positive impact on how it is perceived? Will it be more respected? Loved?

Then the brand will grow and, in time, learn and build its experience. Guided by its core, guided by its very essence, the brand risks struggling to stay true to what it wants to do. It could struggle to find the right middle between its upbringing's ideals and the environment's realities. Like any environment, there are opportunities, uncertainties, openings or misfortunes. Brand aspirations should kindle and rekindle all its reflections and assessments. Without aspirations, the brand could risk stagnating and losing sight of what is next to come or to be done.

A belief system reflects the brand's values. With time, its principles will be guiding many aspects the brand's lifestyle, its business and management styles or its contributions to society. The brand would ask itself "what do I value the most" and "how would that reflect on my significance to others". The brand values shape its personality all externalized actions or interpretations to other members of society. All the brand's DNA constituting elements are reflected through the brand's personality: the way the brand will be speaking, the tone of voice, the language and the perspective it decides to come from when addressing others and being addressed to. The brand makes choices that are related to its physique. It also makes choices related to identifying his friends and flagging those whom he should be looking out from. The brand will be carefully selecting the places where it is going to "hang out" and whom it will be "hanging out with". This will subsequently affect the brand's perception, versus others, in society and the (fashion) retail environment.

Among many hobbies and passions, the brand's main dedication is delivering an offering; physical or non-physical. Throughout its life, it grows toward perfecting the offering, enhancing it, enhancing the way it is delivered and keeping it relevant to those who want to consume it. When the brand needs support and a bigger team to help in delivering its expertise, it will find others who share the same values and have similar dedications. Together, this microcosm of people will consolidate the brand's knowledge, know-how and expertise to deliver a consistent brand message. All brand elements, referred to as the elements of the mix, become undetachable from the brand and work together to preserve its standards. With an eye open and a careful reading of the surrounding environment, the (holistic fashion) brand will be constantly thinking and rethinking its practices, questioning its relationships with actors and seeking best alternatives.

Major changes have upset the fashion retail environment affecting all its actors, including brands. Whether it was a question of sourcing, the choice of materials, the adoption of design software or the integration of a technological aspect that is necessary to the business, brands are going to be affected by the situation. Their objective is not only to survive the turbulent retail environment but to stay true to their identity while taking necessary actions. Questions related to time, cost, money or other currencies, control or substitution are predominant and necessary.

When not working or engaging in commercial/transactional activities, the brand focuses on self-development. It looks at engaging in activities, it pays interest in areas that are not directly related to its expertise and makes sure that its opinions are well heard and understood. Skills and hobbies are outlets to expanding the brand's reach and opening possibilities to practice its skills in areas that are different and new. This gives a sense of freshness and renewal; the brand demonstrates its ability to understand the environment and be more receptive to understanding actors activities in it. Brand interests in new areas open to other societies and to the understanding of what they do and how they function. Authentic, lively and dynamic conversations take place; they knit and interlace different societies of the (fashion) retail environment. An effort to understand everyone's language, to respect each other's opinions and functions makes the brand an engaged and active player.

The significance of physical retail in a fashion retail environment

If physical retail touchpoint functions were considered as main outlets for customer's access to a brand's offering, physical retail would be already on the path to extinction. The fashion retail environment and (fashion) retail touchpoint functions have been undergoing major modifications; they are no longer strictly restricted to procurement, and they have heavily re-integrated the social dimension and experiential dimension into their formats. Today's (fashion) retail touchpoint could be a meeting place, a shopping space, a transitional point of the distribution channel or a communications channel.

We are invited to think of the (fashion) retail format, a previously known distribution channel, as an "access channel". The brand will be putting together all possible relevant channels to simplify the customer's access to its offering and simplify the access to the offering's journey. Despite the complexities of having to integrate several channels, channel types and formats, and despite having to integrate offline, online and ephemeral channels, the customer's experience must be simplified, even, de-complexified.

(Fashion) retail formats would still be doing their intended function with more attention to customers and to their experience. These formats would help customers get closer to their demands and desires and brands closer to their objectives. From an "access retail" channel's point of view, the importance of a retail format lies in its capacity to maintain the balance of the entire chain and assure fluidity of customer movements and interactions with the brand, with each other, in and out of each format, at all times and in any way.

Here is a possible scenario illustrating the new retail realities: while checking her social media site, a customer stumbles on a publication showing a woman in her dress. She clicks on the dress and a link appears on the publication. This action led her to the brand's website and landed her on the page where the dress is displayed. She bought the dress on impulse as she loved it, however, opted for store delivery. Once she receives an email that her order is ready for pick-up in the selected location, the customer heads to the store and asks to try the item before taking it home. She decided to share some pictures on her social media page to ask for her friend's opinions; she tags the brand in the publication she shared. Not having had the answers as fast as she had expected, the customer decides to take the dress home after all. The next day, she re-tries the dress at home and doesn't find it is a good fit. She repacks the dress and prints the necessary provided papers. On her way to work, she drops it off at the post office without any extra charges. A couple of days later, she receives the refunded amount in her bank account.

(Fashion) retail format functions are still the same, their roles, on the other hand, have changed. This change does not jeopardize the brand's strategy, nor question a retail format's performance, only its utility at the right moment in the customer's journey: what the customer will be getting from that touchpoint at that particular time of his journey. On one hand, the physical store, for instance, could be a place for the customer to get in touch with the brand, explore, test the offering and get information from team members. Time and act of purchase might differ and could happen through other channels. On the other hand, the physical store could serve as the place of purchase. After having gathered sufficient information about a brand's product online, the customer heads to the store to try the product and purchase it.

The roles of retail formats are evolving. If we could have thought of a "total product concept", why cannot we think of a "total retail concept"? the total retail concept is to be managed beyond the mere functionality of the format. At first, it considers all possibilities of linking that format to other available brand formats. With the help of technological elements, brand retail formats connect with each other. Customers would enter the brand's bubble at any time from any point and roam its universe by moving from one touch point to the other, engaging with the brand and with others.

Emerging retail formats, like pop-stores, are injecting novelty and a sense of renewal to the (fashion) retail scene. These timely and time-limited stores have given the opportunity to brands to express themselves differently, with greater freedom and with a greater focus on the social dimension of retail. They have reinforced the idea of phygital points that connect the physical and virtual world along with delivering meaningful experiences. The role of the

Total Retail Concept

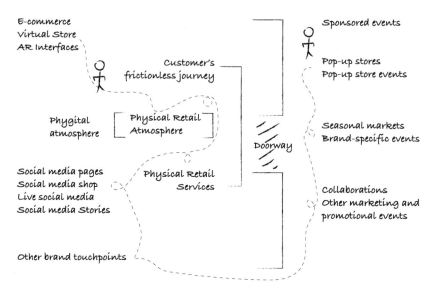

Figure 1.3 The total retail concept

traditional physical store is also changing, and a new meaning is being attributed to it. Offline stores are becoming more experiential, more social and less transactional. As access to any brand's offering could be accomplished through different retail formats, and not restricted to the physical store, brands need to re-design their (fashion) retail spaces to be more immersive, engaging and to give a reason for customers to come over, even do the effort, to visit them.

The physical space is leaning toward becoming a social hub; a place where brands and customers meet and exchange; the transactional dimension is no longer at the heart of this process. Closer to third places than mere retail stores, the physical space is a conversational opportunity were brand and customer share "social quality time". Technology had given the opportunity to re-create and to transpose the physical store online. Whether it is a main store, a flagship or a pop-up that the brand virtually creates,[3] its aim is to make the concept widely accessible, shoppable online and open 24/7. This is yet another reason why the physical store must reinforce its social, immersive and sensory-engaging dimensions.

There was a greater tendency to only consider online stores as e-commerce sites. But online sphere also presents a variety of formats with different functions. Window websites, for instance, are showcase sites that present a brand's products, services or information that it wants to highlight. These websites are closer to institutional sites than transactional sites. It is e-commerce web-sites that have a direct link with conversion; these sites allow internet users, or consumers, to buy and sell physical goods, services and digital products over the internet. As transactional websites suffered from low transformation rates, funnel sites were designed to fulfill that function. Simpler in terms of design but more efficient than traditional e-commerce websites; funnels are dynamic;[4] as if the brand was having a sales assistant guiding each prospect to conver-sion. Social media sites were mainly dedicated to communicating the (fashion) brand's offering. With regular updates, these platforms accommodated func-tions that link the brand's page to its website, e-store, funnel or any other online digital point. Many digital tools that a (fashion) brand installs in its physical store could now be connected to its virtual store, e-store or social media site(s).

This is the era of "holistic retail management"; with retail becoming personal, personalized,[5] connected and reactive, (fashion) retail channels are managed to unify the customer's trajectory and journey by unifying, all reading and opera-tions, of distribution and communications channels. As the retail environment gets more turbulent, (fashion) brands could be constantly put to the test and confronted with changes that they are not ready to adapt to. The challenges are to find the perfect equilibrium between having to keep moving forward adapt-ing to change, and, to the speed of integrating the adopted change.

Fashion Brand Access Topuchpoints

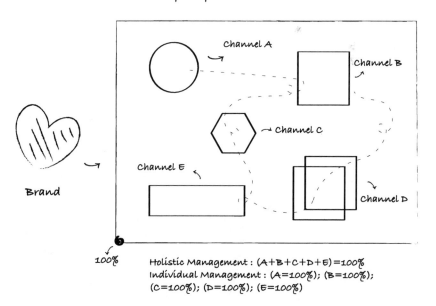

Holistic Management : $(A+B+C+D+E)=100\%$
Individual Management : $(A=100\%)$; $(B=100\%)$;
$(C=100\%)$; $(D=100\%)$; $(E=100\%)$

Figure 1.4 A fashion's brand access touchpoints

Staying true to one's identity

Whether at a conceptual phase, a start-up, a developed or a mature brand, there is the question of relevancy. Can a brand be always relevant on the market? What actions will it take to stay relevant? Would these actions threaten its identity . . . ? how can a brand stay true to its identity in a turbulent retail environment? Moreover, where does the (fashion) brand stand at the consumption process if its relevancy was threatened; would consumers find value in it or in consuming it?

Fashion retail brands would need to make a profit to sustain and survive. Making a living and growing in their environment is only part of their journey. What matters, nonetheless, are decisions that they will be taking to survive. Now, more than ever, profit must be made with integrity and transparency. It is only natural for a brand, business or any individual doing business, to seek a form of return. This, however, could not come at the expense of other brands or consumers, nor at the expense of elements constituting the (fashion) retail and/or the external environment.

The brand must keep educating itself and learning about its environment, its competition and consumers. As an active member of its society, it needs to keep an active conversation with its peers, customers and other interested audiences, an authentic conversation. As consumers are de-consuming, re-consuming or consuming on a toned-to basis, the brand and its offering are no longer relevant to fulfilling its needs. If the brand's sole existence is threatened, then what would become of it? It looks like today's brand is looking for the customer to fulfill its needs: providing ideas or increasing exposure. Consequently, the brand is strengthening its relationships with customers and looking at substitutes and/or supplements to keep maintaining a fruitful relationship.

How to integrate truth and transparency in an exchange process? as the answer to this question is not obvious and there are no guidelines to straightening brand integrity, the best answer would be openness and transparency. All environmental (fashion) retail actors are tightly connected, customers extremely informed and available tools are highly exposing. Through constant actions and honest words, the brand will earn its respect in society; the rest is up to it to keep finding the best ways to keeping the business up and running.

Notes

1. Pettitt, 2016. This hot robot says she wants to destroy humans. Available at: www.cnbc.com/video/2016/03/16/this-hot-robot-says-she-wants-to-destroy-humans.html
2. Posner, 2015. *Marketing Fashion, Second Edition: Strategy, Branding and Promotion.* Laurence King Publishing, p. 240

3. A great example would be that of the "Obsess" whose mission is helping brand turning online shopping into an experience. Please refer to: https://obsessar.com/about/
4. Parkes, 2020. ClickFunnels Vs. Website: Why traditional websites are dying. Available at: www.clickfunnels.com/blog/clickfunnels-vs-website/?gc_id=15306730504&gclid=CjwKCAiA3L6PBhBvEiwAINlJ9FfvA2pkoV3BDAPBMfeo6cS5JGyT3ZlX27Zuh8g7NJtlHzReVDy3bxoCbfIQAvD_BwE
5. Retail technology. Available at: www.retailtechnology.co.uk/news/7639/getting-personal:-retailas-next-chapter/?utm_content=buffer4324b&utm_medium=social&utm_source=linkedin.com&utm_campaign=buffer

Chapter 2

How will retail formats help fashion brands survive?

At times when brand offerings have become very similar across industries and that style, quality or price competition increased, retail formats rose to deliver meaning to purchasing or acquiring products/services. Retail formats are becoming brand's "*porte-parole*" and are participating, more than ever, in liaising between the brand and target audience: their function goes beyond being an element of the brand's mix: it is through the retail format that the brand interacts, exchanges and communicates with customers. Retail formats are also becoming lively; as opposed to "static" retail formats that the Highstreet has witnessed throughout the past decades, today's retail formats are becoming more interactive, everchanging, adaptive of location, of customers or other cultural variables; retail formats mash-in and take part of the retail environment.

In an experiential context, retail environments elevate the meaning from acquiring to owning or even to participating in owning products/services. This chapter focuses on brand retail formats and the choices that must be done to best meet brand strategy and objectives. Keeping the identity at heart, brands can choose from different retail and distribution channels and different formats that these channels might present. Moreover, retail functions are changing, and they do not only cover transactional aspects; they have become places in which customers actively create and produce their experience and hence gain more value from their visit.

With respect to brand objectives, retail formats can be transaction places, third places, experiential spaces, collection points or drop-off points (and this just naming a few of the possibilities). What retail formats to choose and why? How a chosen format should be represented? And What should it include? Moreover, this chapter highlights the importance of physical representations yet contextualizes it among all other brand channels. Retail formats have also become themselves tools for communicating as their format designs or atmospheres, or even the way in which they appear or morph (such as pop-up stores) grasp people's attention and get them talking about the brand.

DOI: 10.4324/9781003173212-3

★(We take another opportunity to thank all fashion brand managers who took the time to share valuable information about their brands)

Retail formats. The brand's *"porte-parole"*

Given the social nature of brand-customer relationships, a retail format is necessary, if not crucial, to present an adequate environment in which the meeting will take place. As part of their social activities, brand and customer both need to interact, engage and socialize; doing so in an adapted location, structures the meeting and formalizes it. Customers get to meet brands in locations that have been developed to serve that particular purpose. For that, an array of physical and digital touchpoints is now available on the (fashion) retail market; each representing a brand and serving its intended function.

Naturally, different fashion brands, at different life cycles, with different capabilities or who seek different retail objectives, accommodate retail formats into their distribution and/or communications channels. At every level of the fashion industry, a brand's strategy considers touchpoints through which and in which it is going to get in touch with customers. Questions concerning the retail format's type, the brand's identity element's manifestation through the retail atmosphere, the attention to customer experience or the extent to which they get to immerse in the environment, are strongly connected to the brand's maturity.

A retail format speaks for the brand; all brand identity elements transmit verbal, non-verbal and sensory messages. The more the brand manages to create a strong network of touchpoints, physical or virtual, the "tighter" the connection built with customers and the clearer the conversation becomes. This being said, a retail format is not only a reflection of the brand's maturity but a reflection of its "health". A healthy brand is one that finds an ideal balance between its management and operations at a certain point in time, given each retail environment and along a specific consumer segment.

Many fashion businesses have emerged during the past decade; to name a few, brands concepts proposing subscription, rental, repair or swapping. Moreover, the great majority were digital native brands and vertical brands. Even though these brands launched online, they have seen themselves personifying their concepts through physical retail formats; whether physical or temporary. Brands realize the extent to which well-designed physical retail environments could engage customers and transform their store journey into an experiential discovery, and a meaningful moment of exchange with the brand. Today's fashion brand retail formats, deliver exceptional experiences when they combine the benefits of online/offline retail and embrace customers by putting them at the heart of the retail touchpoint's journey.

As during any previous era, many players cohabit a fashion retail market. Some are more mature than others, some look at exploring new areas within the industry and others find new opportunities in which they want to invest. Three main brand categories appear in today's fashion retail market. "Newborn brands" are those that emerged during the past five years. They have started as an entrepreneurial business following the footsteps of their elders, or have chosen an entirely different way to kick off with their fashion businesses. Some other brands have been on the market for around a decade; those "developing brands" have managed to confirm their business models and develop their experiences. As they are still malleable and open to change, these brands pay a lot of interest in technologies, infrastructures or techniques that the retail environment presents. The last type of brand, naturally, refers to "mature brands". Those brands having long been on the fashion retail market where they reached a state of stability in terms of performance and all other brand-related aspects. Given the current fashion retail market state, those brands keep an eye open on "newborn brands" as they inspire and provide them with potential avenues for development renewal.

Newborn brands

Today's newborn brands are greatly influenced by this turbulent environment and its actors. Naturally, a new business would rise out of a need or an opportunity, then, find all possibilities to grow and develop on the market. According to its family ties, the way it was brought up and the environment in which it was brought up, a newborn brand's orientations will be made. There is less conformity to what a brand should/should not be as the retail environment has opened greater possibilities to explore a variety of business types on one hand that customers are less formatted into having to accept fewer brand types. This context encourages the development of concepts that are updated, upgraded and unrestricted.

Understanding newborn brands

The turbulent (fashion) retail environment has disturbed an equilibrium that had been long-established between different actors; this led to a change in brand and customer behaviors. On one hand, brands are looking for alternative ways to do business, stay relevant and sustain themselves. On the other hand, customers have become more open, tolerant and forgiving of brand and retail practices. Retail and commerce are slowly going back to simpler forms of exchange, especially when it comes to newborn brands. The exchange and/or transaction process directly takes place between the newborn brand and customer or could happen under the presence of a third party. Many online platforms facilitate and oversee the newborn brand-customer commercial or business relationships. If this relational style has been practiced a century ago under the prevailing market circumstances, it is now being revived and practiced under the current prevailing market circumstances.

There are different types of newborn brands; they stem from an existing business or an existing business model, or simply start as an entirely new (fashion) retail concept. There are undoubtedly difficulties that newborn brands face as soon as they go on the business journey. Depending on the moment during which the concept kicks-off and later the direction it wishes to adopt, it could work on "solo" or "come together" with other brands. With this dynamic, newborn brands are more likely to manifest along others to cooperate and consolidate efforts. This could go from sharing one physical location, the costs of that location, sharing networks, taking advantage of customer dwellings and so on. As such, the (fashion) retail environment accepts more participations and collaborations. Moreover, business relationships within that environment grow to be more supportive and cooperative.

Table 2.1 Newborn (fashion) brand types

Brand type	Definition	Comments
Products/ service brand	– Existing business models/ Existing product our service processes (i.e., a fashion shoes and bags brand using textiles and animal skin). – Existing business models/ New product our service processes (i.e., a fashion shoes and bags brand fish or mushroom skin and alternative finishing details).	Product brands could face problems related to: – Finding raw material and supply – Cost of production and deliveries (and delivery timelines) – Cost of operations (online, offline, stakeholders, teams, customers).
"Nomad" brand	Reviving *an older* retail concept and dressing it up with a modern feel. These brands may present a "retro" style but are very relevant to modern times; they are often services brands (i.e., an individual who bakes his own cakes, brews his own coffee and tours the city with his mobile coffee-truck or a sneaker repair shop who gives a second chance to your pair of shoes).	The business model adopts that more traditional models but presents them in a modern look and feel. "Nomad" brand concepts do not create new concepts, they refresh an older one by making it more relevant to current consumers.

(Continued)

Table 2.1 (Continued)

Brand type	Definition	Comments
"Me" brand	– An individual has a skill, who communicates it on social media and turns it into a business in case of success. – The "me" brand is "the individual"; it represents him at all levels. – The individual multi-tasks and attends to all brand functions: product development, follow up, communications and so on.	To preserve their identity and proximity with customers, these brands would have to stay human-sized. It is okay to sustain by keeping the business at a self-sufficiency level. Shall the brand wish to grow and scale, it might lose their proximity and agility.
Opportune brand	A brand that takes advantage from a retail environmental opportunity to develop its business. The latest technological developments have opened many opportunities for brands to grow mobile, e-commerce or social media-based retail concepts. These brands could be short-lived otherwise, they could morph into different directions. In this case, the brand's creator invests in the acquired skill to develop an enhanced version of the brand. (i.e., drop-shipping websites, coaching, teaching, selling on social media and so on)	If the brand's creator was an amateur, his first "opportunity" could be subject to perfecting. Shall he grasp other opportunities and develop further concept, the outcome will look like mature. Opportune brands could be tightly connected to consumption trends; they would then cater a specific product that meets momentary demand, before moving on to something else.
"Come together" or "fusion brands"	Me brands or mature brands that collaborate for a purpose, to promote a cause or a line of work. Social media platforms have contributed to helping different brands collaborate and communicate their projects.	Finding and maintaining a healthy ongoing relationship with one or many brands.

A newborn brand's values

Today's turbulent (fashion) retail environment questions management and/ or consumption practices. Individuals and professionals have become more aware, awake and more willing to shift to more responsible, engaged and conscious businesses. There is less attention to the product and more focus on the ways of delivering it. Newborn brands values reflect:

- Transparency: non-hidden communications, how it is done? What went wrong? How is the brand fixing it?
- Affinity: members of society who share the brand's values.
- Authenticity: the brand, the customers, the people; one conversation. Uncensored, unformatted. And true.
- Legacy: the brand's actions and decisions that will affect society and the environment.
- Commitment: The brand's promise to enhance and maintain its standards.
- Traceability: the origins of raw materials, stakeholders and members involved in the process of delivering the final product.
- Impact: special attention to the impact that the offering has on the environment (retail, the planet and individuals).
- Quality: delivering what had been promised and with the highest standards.

A newborn brand's structure

If anything characterizes newborn brands, it is that they are human-sized. One person or a very small number of people "are the brand" and manage all aspects of the brand. The initial brand's asset is the conceiver's know-how and skills that he transforms into a form of business. Naturally, different brand structures reflect different newborn brand types; whether it was a "me" brand or an "opportune" brand different structures are required and operationalized. It is very common though to have structure commonalities even if newborn brands are different: "a skill + a tool + a communication method".

For instance, a newborn fashion designer needs her atelier, equipped with a sewing machine, to produce unique dresses. To communicate the offering, a social media platform is adopted. Another example would be that of a digital fashion illustrator who needs a performing computer. If his/her work consists of providing services to fashion companies, he/she could be actively communicating all services on a professional social media platform.

Considerable time and effort are invested before the business takes shape. Moreover, other investments, even if shy, are to be considered if the brand wishes to compete in today's crowded (fashion) retail environment: a visual identity, retail elements (reflecting the visual identity), an online store, a landing page or a funnel page, an active social media page. In a crowded retail environment, a recognizable identity remains one of the most important tools for ensuring brand visibility and recognition. A newborn brand might be ephemeral; in this case, the brand's conceiver detaches itself from the brand. After having created an ephemeral brand, he moves on to another. By this, he would have acquired sufficient knowledge, experience and skills to move on to the next concept with more confidence.

If anything defines a newborn brand, it would be the term "unstructured". This does not mean that the brand is chaotic, it implies that it does not necessarily conform to organizations or methods that define "what a (fashion) brand is and what it should be". If a newborn brand is defined in a universal aspect, it could be linked to an unstructured team or an unstructured brand process and an unstructured retail process. This is not to be "generalized" as, there are cases of newborn brands that adopt aspects from brands that are more confirmed, to accommodate them into their respective models. Moreover, some newborn brands might have extensive knowledge and know-how in one business-related area, but not the other. For instance, a cordwainer displays an ability to design, source and develop a full seasonal collection. He could be less skilled in conceiving a communications strategy or managing his newborn brand's communications online or offline.

Today's (fashion) retail environment gives brands the opportunity to think of developing models that don't conform to the cliché that was long imposed during the past decades. They are not obliged to follow a "pre-designed" way of developing a (fashion) entrepreneurial venture. A newborn brand would develop its own "brand bible" that is personalized and perfectly fits the brand's culture. Whether "learning by mistake" or "organically learning", a newborn brand can perfect its model and preserve its identity through all strategic directions and decisions. If a newborn brand is leaning toward that direction, then the (fashion) retail environment's actors are more open to untraditional ways of doing business with different brands.

At the very essence of a newborn brand's conception, development and management is the process. The process of testing, assessing, retesting and reassessing; continuous trial and error for better decision-making. This process will affect the time and speed of operationalizing the brand and allowing it to have its rightful place on the market among others. A newborn (fashion) brand could not debut on the market without its "starter kit". If an individual lives in a society, he is identified by his affiliations, ownership and physique. Newborn brands are not exempt from taking necessary actions to establish a clear identity, visual identity elements and other tools that serve as identifiers.

Surviving the first period that is essential to "shape up" the newborn brand is essential. Financial and human investments are fundamental; one feeds the other and is necessary to the other. Newborn brands would seek external investments, crowdfunding or secure loans for their projects. There are many cases where newborn brands inject their own finances or gather *love-money* to get their concept started. Excluding product/service brand types, newborn brands are less likely to have the ability to estimate required funds that are needed for the business.

The tight connection between the newborn brand and customers reflects on their relationship and the way they communicate. When they get the chance to physically meet, they get to talk about the brand's offering, quality, likes and dislikes, exchanges ideas opinions and so on. All this information is very valuable to the newborn brand as it helps in shaping and growing it in a direction that meets customer's tastes.

It is more likely that the newborn brand and customer meet virtually, on the social media sites.

It is worth pointing out that communications on newborn brand social media sites don't conform to "classic or traditional communications rules". Content is presented in a textual, photographic, illustrated or video forms that are kept at their rough and initial states. Moreover, options, such as "going live" or keep feeding with "stories" is at the essence. A newborn brands' narrative depends on social media communication, any other media representations and possible physical locations. Eventually, a customer–centric management will incite brands to find ways to keep themselves close to their customers. Time, consistency, coherence and frequency are at the heart of newborn brand communications; this is a challenge to achieve constant visibility and exposure and support sales.

A newborn brand's motto

"Investing in the customer versus investing in the ways to sell to the customer" "respecting the brand's values", "doing what we love, not doing business"

For opportune brands, the motto is more likely to be "grasp the moment and take advantage of it while it lasts"

A newborn brand's distribution and sales

Newborn brands could adopt any distribution and sales formats: personal, physical or online sales. As investment capacities and capabilities are thin at this point of the newborn brand's lifecycle, it could not develop its retail/distribution concept based on an identity, but it does so based on a direction. With the former, the identity, a brand generally follows a long process of translating the brand's ethos into all brand elements, the visual identity and physical evidence for instance. This process is costly, timely and requires many revisions during the first phases of conceptualization. To cope up with this reality, newborn brand takes this first step by developing what they can afford to develop and this following a direction that only aims at reflecting its identity at its best.

Particularities of newborn brand retail and distribution channels is proximity; human proximity. Taking advantage of available of social media platforms, the possibilities of developing online sites or temporary stores, newborn brands redirect their efforts into getting in touch with their customers and potential audiences to start a conversation, exchange information, introduce the brand or promote the offering. Human proximity is characterized by a direct, horizontal, conversation that happens on social media or in physical locations (permanent or temporary). Managing the conversation at this stage is easier because the newborn brand tends to operate a single retail format and couple it with social media communications. Moreover, it cuts intermediaries from the process to keep control over the management process, on one hand, and keep the profit for itself, on the other hand.

The (fashion) retail environment presents brands with an array of retail formats from which they can choose to operate their concepts. A different fashion management school opens new possibilities and pathways for brands to communicate, distribute or engage. Newborn brands have a greater tendency to turn to online formats, social media sites and temporary or ephemeral physical locations. If newborn brands can exist from time to time, why not take advantage of this possibility? If they can get in direct touch with consumers and/to distribute their product directly, why wouldn't they take advantage of this possibility? A simpler, less complicated form of retailing is more reflective of today's newborn brand's managerial direction. Channeled by fashion and retail brand management guidelines, inspired by the metamorphosed retail environment and appealing to a postmodern consumer (or de-consumer), it has regained "soul", become more "human" and less corporate.

Newborn (fashion) brands seek the most convenient alternatives in this turbulent retail environment. Retail touchpoints, physical and online, complete one another; to maintain a constant presence on the market, the newborn brand tends to support its digital presence (that is strongly represented by social media activities) with an online, a physical store or a temporary store. With the costs of managing physical retail operations increasing, operating through concessions, showing in multiband stores, going back to showrooms or sharing physical space with other complementary brands. Temporary retailing, mainly presented by pop-up stores, is the most adopted format.

Pop-up stores are adopted by newborn brands to meet different objectives. On one hand, they can complement social media presence and the online presence. Social media sites have become primary communications and distributions platforms; they direct the customer to the newborn brands' online store and/or directly relate the customer with the brand. To support its communications and retail calendar, the newborn brand injects event-based or commercial pop-up stores. On the other hand, newborn brands adopt pop-up stores on a regular basis to "multiply" other touchpoints (or contact points). To add value to their temporary presence, newborn brand pop-up stores favor unconventional choice of locations, inject events and animations to keep the pop-up store alive and with a "soul".

A pop-up store can be among the first adopted physical distributions channels. As it has become more difficult to opening stand-alone physical locations, newborn brands are looking at many empty physical spaces available on the Highstreet, shopping malls or department stores. If the newborn brand's e-commerce website (or online store) initiates the sales process, a pop-up store ensures closing the sales deal. The pop-up store's human factor assures quality service that adds value to the deal. All choices, related to the point of contact's format and form, reflect that of a localized brand and retail management.

During the first phases of the newborn brand's lifecycle, much effort and attention are turned to getting a potential customer to notice the brand, make a purchase from the brand and contribute to building its journey on the (fashion) retail market. However, a newborn brand wants to keep its integrity and reflect its values through the retail process; instead of imposing its offering, it wants to present it to customers in the most relevant and desirable way at the right moment and in front of the potential audience. Balancing business growth and integrity is no easy decision, but newborn brands are insisting on going back to a human-based management approach.

Newborn brands embrace living in a community; they have seen the value in joining forces with other brands (newborn or more mature) and consumers. With the former, they share mutual benefits, seek greater visibility and learn from each other's experiences. With the latter, they activate a network of people who share the newborn brands' values and advocate them. The newborn not only prefers "human relations", but it also invests in them. It keeps the conversation going, for that, it conceives spaces for exchange. Whether online or physically, all brand touchpoints become exchange points. As newborn brands become more open to receiving and sharing information, they must maintain a straight, clear and unbiased management direction. Given that all newborn brand elements are "in place", the newborn brand will have better chances of success.

A newborn brand's control

As the first steps into the (fashion) retail business is uncertain, the newborn brand keeps the conception-delivery process under its direct surveillance. This helps controlling production and production costs, history keeping for review, tracing and perfecting the business model. In response to today's retail market and today's customer, shortening the production/delivery circuit is in favor by newborn brands. This lets them keep a close proximity with the customer, personalize or customize the offering and involve him in the process of delivering the product. Furthermore, newborn (fashion) brands are thinking more than ever of ways to reduce stock as the costs of raw material, production and deliveries have become unbearable.

Part of controlling the process is keeping production at a close geographical proximity. As the costs of shipping and distribution are increasing, there is less tendency to search for cost-efficient main d'oeuvre. What they aim for is rather the know-how and possibility to deliver the desired outcome that reflects the communicated and expected final offering's value. Going back to working with closer, smaller and more efficient production points (ateliers, smaller factories, tailors, or setting an in-house production) helps the brand minimize stock and, with the right model, accelerate personalized production. Interlaced communications and distributions functions help in tightening the loop between production and distribution. It is becoming more common that newborn (fashion) brands communicate an unproduced style, promote customers to pre-order it (through direct messaging, the mobile application, the website or others) and deliver within the advertised deadline. Hypothetically, all actors of the (fashion) retail environment would also be accepting that state of mind and providing facilitating options to meet newborn brand business management needs.

Table 2.2 Possible newborn brand scenarios

	Communications channel(s)	Distribution channel(s)	Example
Scenario (A)	Social media channel(s)	Direct selling through social media channels	The newborn brand promotes its dresses on its "Instagram" page. It regularly does live product presentations and styling sessions. Customers are invited to contact the brand through "WhatsApp" to request information or purchase.
Scenario (B)	Social media channel(s)	Online shop (or funnel site)	The newborn brand has set up an online store. It promotes the offering on social media channels and directs customers back to the online store.

	Communications channel(s)	Distribution channel(s)	Example
Scenario (C)	Social media channel(s) (and supporting pop-up stores)	Online shop (and supporting pop-up stores)	To support its online store, the newborn brand develops or takes part of a pop-up store. In addition to its communications, it takes advantage of the pop-up store's event to create a conversation and intrigue. The pop-up store helps in temporary sales, reinforces the brand's notoriety.
Scenario (D)	Social media channel(s) (and/or traditional media)	Online shop and physical presence	The newborn brand's online store is supported by one (or more) physical touchpoints, such a concession in a department store or a kiosk in a mall. Many traditional communication tools (in-store communications, press releases, press), coupled up with social media give the newborn brand's customers more information and more options to meet the brand and have access to its offering.
Scenario (E)	Social media channel(s) (and/or traditional media)	Physical store and supporting pop-up stores	The newborn brand's physical presence is supported by pop-up stores and communications (social media and/or traditional). The newborn brand could reinforce its online presence by promoting its physical store and its offering through social media channels (such as "Instagram live" shopping, styling and product presentations.)

(Continued)

Table 2.2 (Continued)

	Communications channel(s)	Distribution channel(s)	Example
Scenario (F)	Social media channel(s)	Pop-up store(s) (and seasonal stores)	Newborn brands lacking capital and operational/ managerial know-how, compensate their physical or online absence by a frequent presence in temporary or seasonal manifestations. They are active on social media and do their best to communicate with customers.
Scenario (G)	Social media channel(s)	Personal selling (and seasonal stores or pop-up stores)	Meeting with the customer one-on-one to present the product and potentially sell it to him/ her. The newborn brand promotes the brands on social media sites and puts much effort in personal communications and networking.

Developing brands

The (fashion) brand has taken the time to learn, relearn and adopt a management direction. At this stage of the developing brand's lifecycle, management processes would have taken their rightful places and contributed to keeping the brand alive. This phase is important for brand's survival and sustainability: it confirms previous decisions and sets initiatives that will help guiding the brand in the future. At this stage, developing brands are still malleable and could shape themselves in ways that are the most relevant to the market and customers. As they have grown out of infancy stages and have not yet matured, they have the aptitude and flexibility to explore possibilities, not from trialing, but an educated decision-making point of view.

Understanding developing brands

After having repeatedly confirmed management processes, a developing brand starts transferring knowledge and know-how at all brand and retail management levels. Team members, infused with the developing brand's culture, employ their skills to best meet and serve its needs. At this stage, team members use available tools and technologies and engage their acquired skills and know-how to enhance the brand's performance.

Table 2.3 Developing brand elements that "sell"

Anchoring the brand	The brand's story: "Who are we, where we came from, what are our aspirations" . . . an individual narrating its story to another (linking it back to its origins, its source)
The brand's culture	The brand's culture contributes to the brand's success; it strengthens ties between brand and customer
"Made by" versus "Made in"	Focusing on the expertise and skill behind the making and not necessarily the location in which it was made
Strengthening brand/customer relationship	Customer-centricity is at the heart of the process
Micro-clienteling	Attending to each customer as if he was the only customer
Keeping everyone informed and in the loop	Communications and brand actions go hand-in-hand; the brand actively and continuously does both

A developing brand also needs to externalize, show-off and increase its visibility. Now that it has confirmed it management processes, it consolidates it efforts to communicating and establishing notoriety. The brand's story plays a central role in its communications campaign; where the brand came from and what are its aspirations? Why does the brand adopt certain decision and not the others? There are no re-creations of fascinating stories as today's developing brands and authentic and real.

The "ways of doing things" shape up a developing brand's culture. Customers grow to understand the brand's personality and relate to its philosophy. They understand the nature of the relationship and how to "deal" with the brand. Together, they share special moments, they share stories and knit a bond. As the developing brand keeps customers involved, their relationship grows beyond that of a transactional nature and more of a friendship.

Developing brand motto

"Exploiting acquired experience to manage the brand while using available tools, platforms and technologies and putting them at the service of customers"

Developing brand communications, distributions and sales

It is seeking ways to enhance and grow that help in developing brands' sustainability. Brand management carefully explores opportunities, online and offline, to meet desired objectives. It is possible to adopt new practices on one hand and to modify, shift or discontinue practices on the other. Much has happened in the (fashion) retail environment over the last decade; fashion brands have faced numerous challenges that are due to all market changes. If they managed to cope with these difficulties, then their decisions were pertinent.

Since 2000, numerous brands, that have developed, crossed the world of electronic commerce. Other brands have surfed the e-commerce wave and started their journey around the dimensions of e-commerce. Whether it is a traditional (fashion) retail brand or an online brand, decisions on communications, distribution or sales of developing brands need to be carefully made.

The integration of social media communications with physical commerce and online commerce, particularly in an omnichannel retail environment, has taken retail to a new dimension: that of channel integration. Developing brands have sought to leverage available social media platforms and all their features to maximize their appearance, communications and conversations with customers; and social media platforms have greatly contributed to that. Even those who were the most reluctant to do it have invested in online presence and social media communications.

Communication functions go beyond information sharing or motivate customers to act. Today's developing brands are looking to strengthen the ties they have forged with their customers. They exhibit a commitment to them and add value to the offer they provide. To demonstrate their good faith, they have adopted several communication tools which bring them closer to their clients and demonstrate their "human" side. Developing brand's social media platform become a source of information, a touchpoint leading to (or commencing a purchase journey) as well as a source of entertainment. Among these newly adopted communications are "live appearances", "live shopping", collaborations with other brands or influencers or bloggers. It could very much organize a well-being and yoga morning session or an evening with a musical brand or a disk jockey.

Social media platforms have been attributed "human" features and physical retail formats have been injected with a span of life. A developing brand that is represented in a multi-brand store, in a concession or in a standalone, is no longer managed as a "retail store". It is now considered as a "living place" (un lieu de vie): a place of exchange, a place to meet, a place of expression. There is a greater tendency to encounter other brands that are consistent with the developing brand's activities. Such brand communities invest in collective efforts and outsource their communications by emphasizing on storytelling. Moreover, they tend to entertain customers through a continuous events calendar. This customer-centricity and investment in the human side of the developing brand has also taken advantage of the advent of pop-up retailing. Pop-up stores are conceived, and very much dedicated to the final consumer. Event-based pop-up stores help developing brand in meeting their objectives; those closely related to getting in direct contact and entertaining consumers.

Developing brands consider their physical environment as a place of networking and a great way to build up connections. Having a physical location, better be a main location, helps brand managers meet those goals. When having a permanent physical location is less likely, turning toward pop-up stores, concessions or taking part in multi-brand stores is their reasonable option. Moreover, when developing brands look at exploring new locations, markets or areas to develop, they feel that pop-up stores are suitable. There is a tendency to associate developing brands' lack of financing, to grow through physical locations, with the idea that they are fully developed e-commerce; this is unfortunately not the case.

As physical, temporary and digital retail formats require considerable investments, developing brand managers take careful steps before venturing in one retail format or the other. A physical store requires attention to stock and human capitals, their management, communication costs versus the potential of transforming their stock. There are no concessions related to investments when it comes to online stores. The absence of a physical retail store's tactile atmospheric elements does not imply a lower investment; in this case there are other costs related to managing the website; its back end; software, managing account, payments or securing servers.

Mature and established brands

Understanding a mature or established brand

Heritage luxury brands and emblematic services-industry brands are excluded from this classification. Being on the market for more than a century elevates a brand. They become a reference, a guide: Hermes, Asprey, the Ritz London, the Georges V or the Plaza. They set standards and points of reference that are used as benchmarks that mature or developing brands aspire to achieve, and that start-up brands inspire from.

Mature (fashion) brands and businesses are those who established notoriety and reached a higher level of visibility. They secured their spots on the fashion retail market and in the retail environments. Mature brands find themselves on the target audiences' top-of-the-mind lists, they are taken "more seriously" by other businesses and stakeholders. A mature brand's dynamic is very much different than that of newborn or developing brands. It studies the environment, benchmarks, anticipates and proactively acts. A "real-time" market watch keeps the brand focused, alert and ready to move toward the next step. Now that it values its strengths and looks at ways to enhance its weaknesses, mature brands have quicker reflexes in grasping openings and opportunities.

After having lived long enough on the market, ventured in opportunities, reevaluated their objectives and realigned with the market, mature brands take a step back. Now that they have witnessed success, difficulties, struggles or even failures, they have a greater ability to look for their next move and what to stay away from; the brand's identity remains the main reference and driver. In fact, mature brand managers are more affirmative and can know when the best time is to stop, revise or change direction. Their anticipation and reflexes push them to make immediate and informed decisions.

Mature brands are also confronted with a moment when they must reinvest in their human and physical capitals. This non-negligible cost is inevitable yet necessary. To stay relevant, mature brands seek ways to inject freshness and renew into their business models.

- They rethink their current processes and adopt more responsible actions that have a positive impact on customers and the fashion retail environment.
- They might grow into complementary businesses or extend their offering.
- They might invest their efforts to acquire a new market and a new audience.
- They catch a rising opportunity and shift the business' model or the approach to doing business.
- They accommodate the business and its model to what customers expect and what makes them feel more comfortable.
- They get inspired from the retail environment and from newborn brands.

A brand's perception might differ from one market to another. Even if a brand has achieved maturity in a given market, it does not make it eligible to receive the same welcome among other markets. This being said, there is a thin line between a band's perception as a "fashion brand" or a "fashion business". Depending on the customers individual personality traits, their culture, backgrounds and fashion brand education, they are inclined to categorize and associate a fashion brand, to its owner/designer, or compare it to other businesses providing fashion-related product/services.

Mature brand key variables

Among mature brand types we present those that are personalized and non-personalized. In both cases, the human factor is very much present and has a strong impact on the brand-customer relationship.

- "Personalized mature brands" are those offering their customers the possibility to custom or personalize their products

- "Non-personalized mature brands" are those providing a clear offering without a possibility to personalize it. Services, on the other hand, could very much be personalized.

In addition to the close proximity that mature fashion brands have with their customers, they invest in:

- Services: All aspects relate to the access to the product, its delivery and after sales services.
- Interactions: The brand's attendance to customer needs, meeting his/her expectations and keeping an ongoing conversation between them.
- Product quality and signature style: The brand commits to conceiving, developing and delivering unique styles and a quality that reflects its identity and meets customer's expectations.
- The physical sphere: The mature brand's physical environment is an important, if not a major element, to represent and reflect the brand. In addition, portraying the brand's universe and making the offering accessible, the physical sphere (stand-alone, concept store, concession, pop-up store or other formats) ignites the brand/customer conversation in a reserved sphere.
- The digital sphere: Online presence has grown to externalize the brand's image and expand its reach. During the pandemic, it helped brands stay in touch with their customers and keep promoting the offering. The digital sphere has grown even further; it informs about the brand's activities and potential expansions in the metaverse or its development of new offerings, such as the NFTs.

Mature brand distribution and sales

Mature brands, like other types of brands, adopt one or more retail formats. Adopting and investing in physical locations remains at the heart of their distribution strategies. A physical location "affirms" the brand's presence, "marks" its identity and keeps it at close distance with customers. Mature brands that can invest in physical locations could attribute different functions to each of them. For instance, attracting attention on the product to encourage and facilitate transactions. The physical location could also be a meeting place; brand representatives and customers find themselves building a positive and trusting relationship. More importantly, mature brands think of the relationship as being able to take the business to the next level. At times when the (fashion) retail market is saturated and the offering is no longer an element of differentiation, the human factor, that is much attended to in a physical location, becomes an added value to the brand.

Physical locations could be boutiques, showrooms, physical representation in department stores. Mature brands invest in physical stores to gain better exposure and more visibility. Department store and pop-up stores remain the brand's preferred outlets to meet those objectives. For digital native brands or online businesses that have been successfully gaining their places on the market, manifesting in physical locations, whether permanent or temporary, is evidence to the importance of this format, especially when it comes to brand/customer relationships.

With mature brands, business development is not linear. Growth is very tightly connected to environmental circumstances that present opportunities or signals many threats. The focus should remain on finding an ideal state that balances choices related to the (fashion) brand's notoriety, the brand's offering and the brand's sales. Physical locations must keep the brand aligned with these objectives at all times.

Mature brand communications

Mature brand communications became more consistent over time. Consistency in timing, style, content and message. Communications are as costly as any other brand touchpoints but are managed as being brand investments: they keep customers informed, they convey the brand's identity and speak on its behalf. With mature brands, communications are equally present in the physical store, on social media and through traditional media outlets. The closer the brand is to a luxury positioning, the higher the investments in personal communications. Physical retail environments are great ways of communicating. Mature brands invest in storytelling to transfer the brand's story (or a part of it) and to give customers the opportunity to co-construct their own experience throughout their contact with the brand physical touchpoint. In-store design elements, whether presented in a physical or digital formats, remain integral part of these environments.

The advent of social media (circa 2008) played a key role in developing (fashion) brand exposure. More than a decade ago, social media was a "thing"; intrigued with this platform and its potential, many (fashion brands) dare to invest them. Social media pages presented the opportunity to showcase and promote a brand's products. More recently, showcasing became a fraction of what this sphere could offer; with social media, the brand exchanges with its community and actively keeps the conversation going. Exposure on social media helps the brand extend its reach. From celebrity endorsements to collaborating with bloggers and influencers, social media has greatly contributed to reinforcing the mature brand's identity.

Mature (fashion) brands attribute a new meaning to communications. It is about keeping an active conversation among brand community members. Community members represent the brand's heart and soul and keep the dynamic flowing. Communications, in these turbulent times, is a conversation; communications channels assure the transition of information by/between the brand and community members.

A mature and established brand's motto

"The ability to adapt, the facility to adopt and the power to influence"
   "Putting ego aside is the way to having a clear state of mind and success-ful, sustainable brand"

Table 2.4 Newborn versus established brands

	Newborn brand	Mature/established brand
Brand	Knowledge Know-how Available resources Exploiting resources Ability to learn and relearn	Has a clear identity and a clear positioning Has built a connection with customers Has recognition in the fashion retail environment
Value	The value customers see in the brand Customer's willingness to exchange against money, time and effort	The value customers gain for maintaining a connection with the brand (being part of the brand's circle)
Quality	Whether the final offering meets the brand's identity and its initial proposition	Consistent delivery of the offering over time
Time	The amount of time that is needed to deliver	Brands' relevancy in a context and at a particular time
Timing	The ability to deliver on time	Timing is at the essence of all brand actions (ranging from design, production to communications)
Relevancy	Trial, testing and error Organic growth Survival	Assess Evaluate Take action Reevaluate
Retail formats	Existing to "exist" Needing to affirm presence on the market The retail format is considered as brand distribution point and a customer acquisition channel	Creating opportunities to meet, engage and exchange with customers The retail format becomes a differentiating brand tool The brand's access to products/services is a result
The retail environment	The retail market's infrastructure plays a key role on the brand's development and growth. The retail market's infrastructure also unveils many opportunities that brands could grasp, if well prepared and ready to. Customer culture, education, degree of acceptance, confidence and perception toward (fashion) brands affect the brand's sustainability.	

The significance of space in a fashion retail context

Brands recently saw themselves taking immediate action to closing physical retail stores that became burdening. Only those outlets that were profitable were kept. In today's unified commerce context, brands align their process with different adopted retail channels to keep the customer's journey fluid. Physical retail channel's functions, such as the stand-alone boutique or pop-up store, are not limited to presenting merchandise or selling. What use for a physical store if its functions are simply those of accessing a product? what use for a physical store if customers won't mobilize their effort to get there?

Retail formats and their roles in today's fashion retail environments

Many physical retail concepts have emerged after the 2008 recession. Characteristics that they share with the physical store are restricted to atmospherics dimensions. What is most interesting however are their functions: Fore and foremost, these physical stores reflect a clear concept. They are places meeting, discovery, exchange and a place where stories are told. They are somewhere between a communications gallery, a museum and a physical point of sale. In addition, the objective of such space is to initiate customer experiences. An interesting retail business model appeared with the development of these concepts; the space is rented for a brief period to a given (fashion, traditional or digital native) brands or to a group of complementary brands. The *experiential store's* team vouches to provide all necessary services to the resident brand. It presents its identity, provides a playground of immersive experiences and assists in its communications.

Table 2.5 Customer involvement in different retail locations

	Non-physical location	Experiential and experimental physical location	Legitimate physical location
Less experiential	A purely function relationship of information/ product acquisition	Receptive and attentive to information that he/ she acquires from the environment	Less involved. The customer's involvement is strictly for procurement
More experiential	The possibility to project oneself into the presented universe	Actively engages in co-creating his/her experience	Very much immersed and projects himself/ herself in the themed/theatrical space

The (fashion) brand's presentation at this *experiential store* is a tool to communicate a story and narrate it to its community and potential customers. A (fashion) brand, it has now an array of touchpoints in which it can manifest to come closer to its community: physical stores, digital stores and alternative reality stores. It completes, links and soften the transitions between these touchpoints to provide an exceptionally fluid customer experience. It is highly likely that a given (fashion) brand would choose to be temporarily present at an *experiential store* to meet an objective or purpose. Most importantly, brands take advantage of the adaptability and agility of these *experiential stores* to configure the space and tailor events to meet their needs.

Atypical retail, such as these *experiential* and *experimental stores* are very difficult to position among other retail formats. They are not classic physical retail formats, nor pop-up stores, nor a marketplace. If they need to be categorized, they must be presented as being *relational experiential stores* that put customers at the heart of any and every decision and action. Individuals have never stopped evoking their desire to seeing, touching, feeling, testing, trying and meeting others during their shopping and consumption journey. Therefore, these retail touchpoints keep customers and the customer experience at the heart of their model.

Today's physical retail stores reawaken the beauty of traditional touchpoints. They are lively and alive. They are experiential and experimental. They are personal and social. They are transactional and non-transactional. They are no longer supply points; they have become reception points where the offer is not the only thing that customer receive. Human interactions are the physical store's engine brand representatives, potential customers and clients engage in an ongoing conversation and exchange of information. A brand/customer proximity starts at the physical point of sale, then grows and develops on other brand touchpoints. When the brand re-directs the flow toward another physical touchpoint, whether *experiential* or more

Table 2.6 Physical space's utility for product or experience brands

	Product brands	*Experience brands*
Reflects	The brand's know-how	The brand's experience
Focuses on	The brand's skills	The brand's story
Ranges (from-to)	Low-end → more available	Less exceptional → more accessible
	High-end → less available	More exceptional → less accessible
Physical space	Serves a purpose	Is a state of expression
The offering	Highlighting the available and displayed offer	Promoting the act of accessing the available offer or
Physical space's utility	Completes an act of acquisition	A space of expression and/or self-expression

traditional, it seeks keeping the energy and dynamic. (Fashion) brands are paying attention to each touchpoint by re-humanizing all retail aspects, even the most function or utilitarian ones.

Physical, digital, experiential, ephemeral to human touchpoints. At times when brand management grew to invest in the retail store's atmosphere, offline and online, in the offering or in the experience, it realized the extent to which it should invest in humans. This is a currency that will yield positive outcomes to brands and will elevate them to become more human. Going back to the brand being a person, it is only natural that it flaunts its human qualities to stay true to oneself and its beloved.

How will retail formats help fashion brands survive?

In today's turbulent retail environment, physical retail will help brands stand on their feet, as they will redirect them toward the essence – customers.

- Physical retail is becoming agile, mobile and more flexible: brands are finding new retail formats and redesigning retail spaces that are easier to manage, modulate and move to around. They add more dynamic and inject life into the retail function.
- Physical retail will get brand and customers together. Gatherings are convivial, happy and conversational.
- Physical retail will strengthen brand–customer relationships.
- Physical retail will re-enforce customer's presence and keep them at the heart of the brand's equation.
- Physical retail will tell a story in which customers are protagonists.
- Physical retail will reinject meaning into the brand's "raison d'être".
- Physical retail will be intimate.
- Physical retail will stay away from "odd places" and be closer to "cool places".
- Physical retail will stay away from conglomerate retailing and will rekindle hometown shopping.
- Physical retail will design the right "context" to get in touch with customer and focus on rebuilding personal connections.
- Physical retail will be re-humanizing the shopping experience.
- Physical retail will be humanizing the act of purchase.
- Human link + human proximity.
- The store will reinject meaning in the brand's existence.
- Exhibit versus display.
- Appears during times and at places that are relevant to customers.
- Data collection point that is real, authentic, engaging.
- Retail formats are the start of a brand's customer journey.
- Retail formats are the result of a brand's customer journey.
- A place where knowledge, know-how, experience, thoughts and feelings are exchanged.

Newborn brands

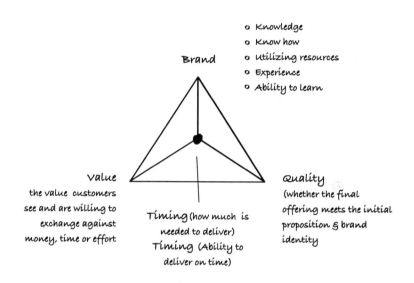

Brand
- Knowledge
- Know how
- Utilizing resources
- Experience
- Ability to learn

Value
the value customers
see and are willing to
exchange against
money, time or effort

Timing (how much is
needed to deliver)
Timing (Ability to
deliver on time)

Quality
(whether the final
offering meets the initial
proposition & brand
identity

Established brands

Have an advantage over new borns as they are :
Taken more seriously by customers & businesses
Given more support from businesses

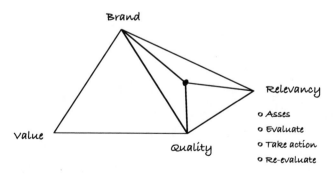

Brand

Value

Quality

Relevancy
- Asses
- Evaluate
- Take action
- Re-evaluate

Figure 2.1 Newborn brands versus established brands

Chapter 3

The fashion brand spectrum
Scenarios for success

Different brand categories operate at different industry levels. This chapter presents scenarios for different types of fashion brand operating at different brand levels (mass, masstige, ready-to-wear, designer, luxury and so on). It puts forward different scenarios indicating a starting point, leads, look-outs, staying away from menaces or embracing opportunities that are presented along the way.

With every brand and at each brand category level, management is different. Each brand is very different from the other, very much like individuals, and has different capabilities and requirements than the other. Brands with a similar positioning and a similar offering, that compete for the same market share and the same target audience, have been through very different routes to reach that point. Every brand has been through different paths and situations. There are no certainties that a (fashion) brand follows "one right way" to develop and grow.

Fashion brands cater their offering at different market levels to meet with the needs of different types of audiences. The simplest example is that of a white T-shirt that you can find at the price of 1$ in a fast-fashion store and at 200$ at a high-end fashion store; the brands operating at these two stores cater to different audiences and have different brand strategies. Given the fact that this T-shirt is produced at the same factory, with the same machines and the same fabric, what makes its value and worth so different? is it the way the brand presents itself, the story behind it, or how customers perceive it? Some brands operating at the lower level of the spectrum might "inspire" from others operating at the higher level of the spectrum to increase the brand offering's value and others might propose lines and can decide to project them as "more affordable" to cater to a greater audience. What can the brand do, to what extent it can "borrow or inspire" from other brands and what should it be thinking of in order not to "hurt" its identity and positioning on the market? This chapter aims at putting forward different routes that brands could think of to move up, down or across market levels, and looks at possible ways in which it can physically appear and manifest in front of the target audience.

DOI: 10.4324/9781003173212-4

Different fashion brands. Different management scenarios

First the recession and then the pandemic. A decade full of changes, challenges and uncertainties. The fashion retail environment, pre and post pandemic, have revealed many realities related to management flaws and fortes. If fashion retailers have learned one thing, it would be that managing is personal to each. Each brand acts, reacts, learns, unlearns, integrates, associates and takes decisions differently. This is very similar to learning during early childhood; for some, learning to speak faster is easier than taking their first steps. Each at his own pace and his own time. There are certainly codes and standards of the fashion retail market. Whether start-up or mature brands, whether catering to mass or luxury markets. Today's management is in desperate need of a breath of fresh air. It requires openness, a degree of acceptance of change and the willingness to unlearn only to relearn and move forward.

As customers grew tired of formatted retail, they followed those brands that managed to mesmerize them. Fashion brands that failed applying changes to meet customer expectations have found themselves forsaken and became less relevant. Others that saw their ways through, whether they have been on the fashion retail market for a long time or are still very new to it, captured consumer's attention. They directed their efforts toward the customer and look at all possible ways to get in touch with that customer in today's turbulent fashion retail environment, nothing makes more sense than investing in the human factor. This does not only consist of being customer-centric, but to integrate the customer in all aspects of the brand and keeping him in the brand's loop. Are customers to be considered as brand stakeholders and influencing brand members?

How can brands be active members of the fashion retail society?

Similar to any member of an active society, a fashion brand's lifetime is a journey of self-discovery, growth, success, failures or opportunities. If today's fashion brands want to become active members of the fashion retail society, they will have to look out for their well-being and that of their environment. As active members of their society, brands are invited to have an open mind to sharing, contribution and investment: first, sharing their know-how, skills or information in a way that is useful to society. Then, actively contributing to making society a better place; through internal practices and responsible business actions. Finally, investing in the human and environmental capital to have a greater value to people and the business.

Fashion brands are invited to be the best versions of themselves. This exercise requires an evaluation of the self and an evaluation of how the self

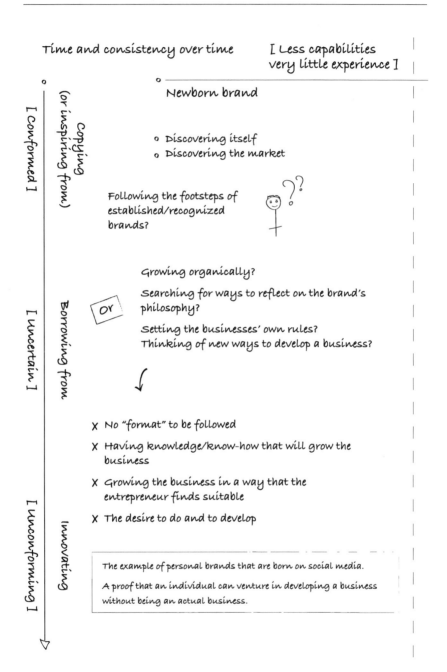

Figure 3.1 A fashion brand's relevancy over time

[Capability
& experience]

Established brand

Mature brand

o Survived ant foot in the
  market
o Tried, repeated and conformed
  a clear process

o Reputation
o Recognition
o Reference
  (international/global)

Contentment with current
(positive) results & brand
performance

Inject novelty
& innovate its
concept?

Expect more of the
brand need to rethink
the current process

The business is
operational
The brand is recognized
(and has high equity)
The business model is
clear (internally and with
stakeholders)

Could it be the themed and
theatrical points of sales?

Could it be communications &
conversations?

Could it be events &
entertainment?

o A brand procedures book
o A standardized process
o A clear guiding business
  model

If satisfied,
would you scale?

X Confronted to the market
X Confronted to the environment
X Confronted to customer
  changing/shifting behaviors

The example of personal
brands that are born on
social media.
A proof that an
individual can venture
in developing a
business without being
an actual business.

Entrepreneurial venture
with potential to
complete/support the
recognized business

Seeks ways to
innovate, refresh

Has an eye open on the market,
market trends, competition &
new businesses

Copy an entrepreneurial
brand's concept and "force it
out one the market"

Unconforming brand
Rebel brand

would benefit others and the environment. Fashion brands should flaunt their personal traits and individualities to portray a stronger version of the self. They are to complete other brands, not compete with them. They are to complement what other brand lack, not overshadow them. If retailing has been promoting "bigger is better", today's fashion retail brands are invited to think of the statement "together is better".

This era of contradiction and divergences has shaken the very essence of fashion retail management. New communications and distribution channels have appeared; they provided fashion retailers the opportunity to explore unconventional tools, and to customers, they gave hope and a breath of fresh air. For instance, giant online fashion retailers and digital native vertical brands adopted temporary or pop-up physical locations. A wave of local entrepreneurs reinhabited hometowns and the local highstreets. New concepts of alterations, repairs or made-to-order and are reappearing; these concepts have rematerialized into modern looks. Digitalizing physical stores, or physicalizing e-commerce sites, promoting on social media or sponsoring a local event have become the norm. Fashion brands are also finding new ways to get in touch with customer, their environment and even other brands, whether from the fashion industry or not.

Fashion retail brands are exploring their environments and experimenting areas which do not necessarily belong to the field of fashion. Instead of abiding by a set of dictated norms, today's fashion brands do whatever they think is right, if they stay true to their identity. There is no longer an exception to what to adopt; rather, fashion brand adapts to unforeseen circumstances or situations by resorting to new possibilities. All these efforts were to get closer to the consumer and to give meaning to the act of consumption.

Fashion brand toolkits and scenarios

Personal fashion brands and young designer brands

A personal determination and a precise personal idea make up a personal brand. The main drive to start on a personal brand journey is to get off the beaten tracks of formatted fashion brands. They have a positive vision of the world and wish to have a say or reflect their own ideas through products or services. Personal brands are also driven by principles; their brands should be an answer or a solution to a prevailing problem. For example, A personal fashion brand catering to conscious parents and who are not comfortable with excessive spending on newborn garments. The brand develops *transformative* organic cotton garments. Another personal fashion brand creates jewelry out of recycled gold or silver. To stand for women and empower them through its fashion, a personal brand employs a video strategy to transmit her voice to those who are share the same values.

Personal fashion brands management is unique. It does not follow existing managerial guidelines, nor sets up a management process to start and grow its brand. It has its own dynamic and own way of doing. Very much guided by the founder's personality and principle, a personal fashion brand is/looks at:

- Solving a problem through in-depth research and investigation: the personal brand must have a meaningful purpose;
- Taking time to secure sources to ensure the project's feasibility: Product, sourcing, price, manufacturing, source/origins/transparency of materials;
- The ability to involve customers in the process: finding ways to share relevant information that customers value;
- The difficulty to outshining, competing with the high number of other personal brands (or other fashion brands) on the market;
- Renouncing all forms of strategic guidance. These "free-souls" want to succeed at their own terms.

What prevents personal fashion brands from taking-off? And what holds back their development and growth? It seems like personal brands are foretold to death from the start:

- With regards to their business model, they are closer to being artisans.
- They are not organized nor have organizational qualities. They also retract from those who try to structure their work process.
- They are not consistent. Whether in production patterns or communications matters, personal brand managers are far from the notion of committing to time frames or deadlines.
- Their ideologies overshadow their business spirit.
- They lack financing or any financial support.
- They tend to get into the wrong associations as opposed to choosing the right partner.

It is apparent that personal fashion brand founders are guided by their emotions, which prevents them from seeing right from wrong. There are many elements preventing the business from developing; but again, are these brands looking to be compared to other fashion brands? Are we looking at the right indicators to measure their success or failure?

Young designer brands might share similarities with personal fashion brands, such as staying focused on one way of doing things or being blinded by emotions. moreover, young designers are less agile and less flexible with their approach of managing their brand. Finally, they risk being caught up in the *exploration* loop. Many young designers feel that they must yet explore other ways to perfect their product and lose sight of everything relating to the brand's promotion.

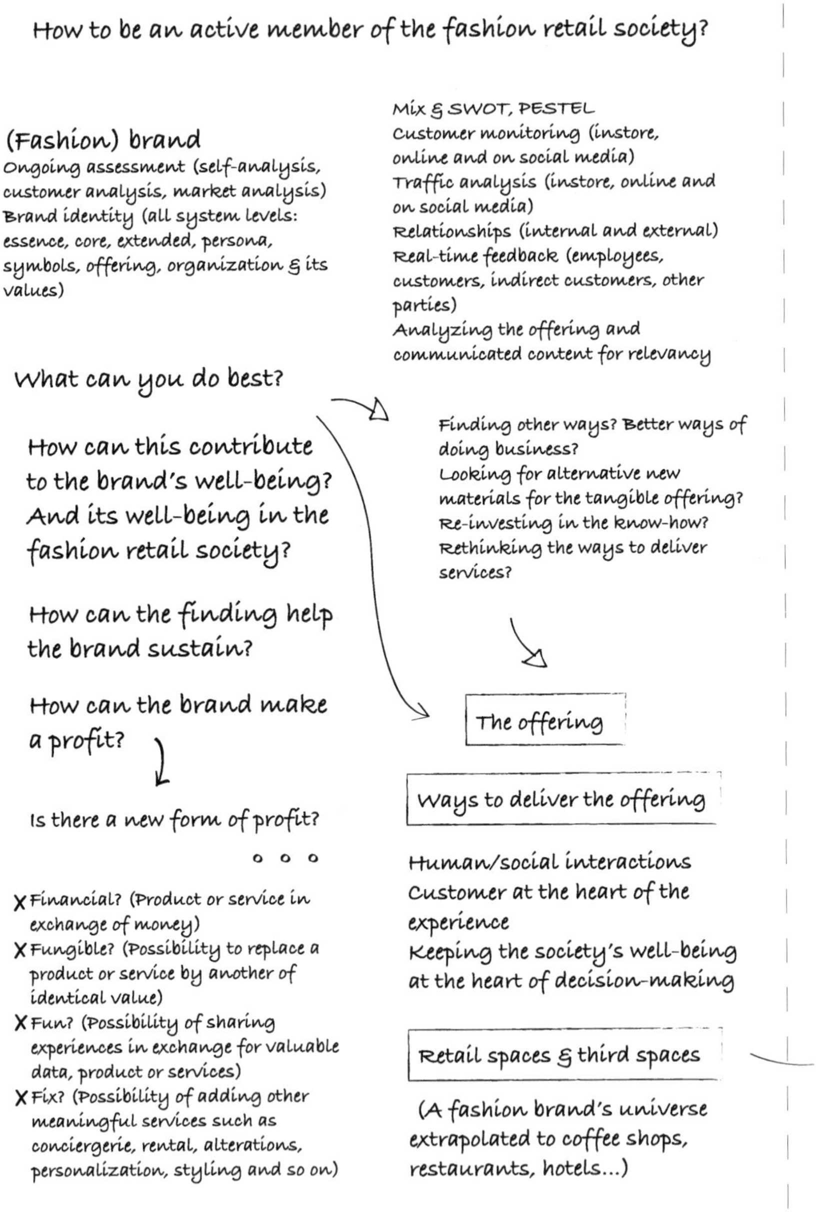

How to be an active member of the fashion retail society?

(Fashion) brand
Ongoing assessment (self-analysis, customer analysis, market analysis)
Brand identity (all system levels: essence, core, extended, persona, symbols, offering, organization & its values)

Mix & SWOT, PESTEL
Customer monitoring (instore, online and on social media)
Traffic analysis (instore, online and on social media)
Relationships (internal and external)
Real-time feedback (employees, customers, indirect customers, other parties)
Analyzing the offering and communicated content for relevancy

What can you do best?

How can this contribute to the brand's well-being? And its well-being in the fashion retail society?

How can the finding help the brand sustain?

How can the brand make a profit?

Is there a new form of profit?

○　○　○

✗ Financial? (Product or service in exchange of money)
✗ Fungible? (Possibility to replace a product or service by another of identical value)
✗ Fun? (Possibility of sharing experiences in exchange for valuable data, product or services)
✗ Fix? (Possibility of adding other meaningful services such as conciergerie, rental, alterations, personalization, styling and so on)

Finding other ways? Better ways of doing business?
Looking for alternative new materials for the tangible offering?
Re-investing in the know-how?
Rethinking the ways to deliver services?

The offering

Ways to deliver the offering

Human/social interactions
Customer at the heart of the experience
Keeping the society's well-being at the heart of decision-making

Retail spaces & third spaces

(A fashion brand's universe extrapolated to coffee shops, restaurants, hotels...)

Figure 3.2 How to be an active member of the fashion retail society?

Rethinking retail distribution ⟶ Boundaryless retail ° ° °

X Customers will get their product from brands and channels that offer something "extra" and for "less" money/effort.

X Retail distribution, that grew alongside e-commerce, gave access to product: easier and faster.

X A retailer's, or a re-seller's, competitive advantage has changed: it is not the offering, but the way in which the customers will access it and how will it add value to their experience. Instead of communicating a competitive advantage the brand portrays its personal traits.

Diluted retail experience
Decomposing the act of shopping
The act of shopping could happen anytime, anywhere and through any device

Reinventing retail concepts
Magazine stores
Online rental physical retail spaces
Experimental brand labs

Relevancy
Making sense to customers and to the retail environment
Responding to customer needs
Reflecting customer current states

Evidence
Customers want "realness"
Physical retail is "proof" of what the brand claims

Connected & engaging
Local or reflects local environmental aspects
Attends to local customer needs & expectations
Gives something back to society

Autonomous
Automated retail concepts
Vending machines
Self-service, self-checkout stores
Connected stores
Concepts that are self-sufficient and less dependent on third parties

Physical space to action
Action to physical space
A location that is promoted online entices customers to go and visit it.
The area surrounding that new "destination" is revived.
(Example of movies/television series and their impact on fashion brands, services brands and physical locations)

However, there are major differentiating points related to their business savviness:

- They have a clear vision of who they are, what they stand for and what message they want to send out to their targeted audience.
- They put an effort into formalizing their artistic know-how into easily marketable offering.
- They seek reference retail channels to promote their offering (online and offline).
- They understand the importance of experience in the retail context. They have non-conformist approaches to presenting their offering in physical or online stores. They also have a great tendency to collaborate and join efforts with other brands, artists or illustrators.

How could personal brands and young designer brands stay authentic and true in this turbulent fashion retail environment?

By investing in what they know and what they can do best.

By looking at ways to enhance themselves and not ways to try to resemble others.

During these turbulent times, personal and designer brands are to refocus and recenter their efforts. They need to find their ways of being methodically consistent. This must be reflected through all brand actions, whether product presentation, communications or activities. Members of the fashion retail environment, consumers and stakeholders, are reassured when they engage with consistent brands. Consistency is not confused with dullness or lack of creativity. Brands that are looking at ways to best manage during these turbulent times, are to choose any action that respects its identity and is in line with its values.

Three pillars for growing personal brands and young designer brands: offering, communications and associations. The offering must reflect the brand's identity, be relevant to and in line with customer's expectations; it does not have to be large, wide or varied. What matters is that a particular brand's offering makes sense to customers and that they see value in it. Once the brand is clear on its offering, it must communicate it. It also must communicate how it has made it readily available to consumers. Most importantly, it must get into an active communication process with those who have consumed it or still hesitating. Instead of being restricted to promoting the offering, communications should be narratives that inviting customers to the brand's world. To maintain the dynamic and keep the conversation going, personal brands and young designer brands are expected to associate. This association manifests in different aspects and at different levels: it could be a design association, it could be teaming up in retail-related projects, it could be a way to explore new or complementary businesses.

While both brand types share many similarities, it is worth highlighting that young designer brands do have to inject novelty in their offering: at a conceptual level, design level, the product's finishing and materials used to deliver the final product. they are to pay much attention to sourcing and the nature of raw materials and accessories that they are going to use to deliver that final product. Engaging with stakeholders and partners who share the same brand values is a must. What brands should keep in mind is that their strength lies in understanding their limitations. Opening to other brands, businesses and to consumers is sign of goodwill. It is an indication of readiness to growing into a better version of the self, for the benefit of the fashion retail society.

Newborn fashion brands

A newborn, start-up fashion brand, like many other industry start-ups, live the journey of obstacles, hiccups, struggles and stress. Rare are the cases when a start-up brand sees having satisfying results during its early days. Right after the journey commences, start-up brand founders find themselves solving enigmatic and challenging situations. The founder's state of mind must be open to assessing, reassessing, revising, repeating, questioning, taking risks, trying, experimenting and validating. It employs a set of skills to conceive an idea, then, with limited resources, it sees ways to best shape the concept. The newborn brand's journey starts by surrounding itself with people, organizations and mentors who are of guidance and help. The entourage plays a vital role at this phase; it should provide all the infrastructure that is needed to help the brand in concretizing. It is not a surprise to see many start-up brands gather around in incubators, regularly meet-up during conventions, gather around fairs, trade shows or exhibitions.

- The founder: in most cases the founder has the vision and an acceptable level of knowledge (and know-how) with regards to the field that it wants to start-up at. The confrontations between theoretical knowledge and market knowledge reflect the start-up environment's reality. To have a better chance of succeeding in today's retail environment, the newborn brand's founder must have the willingness to test, make mistake, learn, develop, assess, act and reassess. If/and when surrounded by experienced mentors, the trial-error period and most possible risks are considerably reduced. The learning curve is enhanced over time and helps speed up the newborn brand's development. For instance, a newborn fashion brand led by an experienced founder has greater, and faster, chances to develop than that let by a novice founder.
- The network: the newborn brand will have a hard time developing without a network. It is with these individuals, mentors, collaborators and associations that it will set its foundations. Associating with

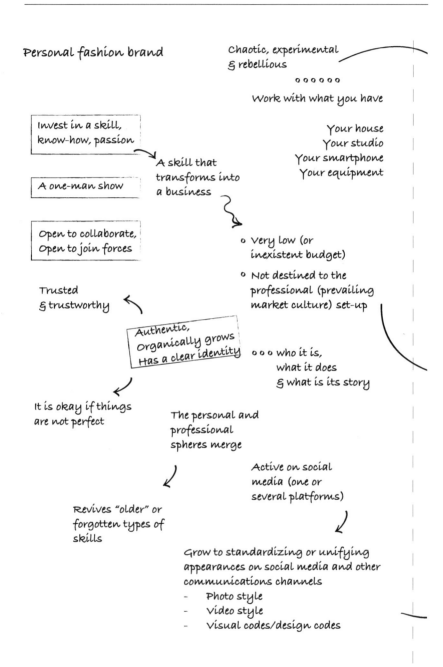

Personal fashion brand

Chaotic, experimental & rebellious

o o o o o o

Work with what you have

Invest in a skill, know-how, passion

Your house
Your studio
Your smartphone
Your equipment

A skill that transforms into a business

A one-man show

Open to collaborate, Open to join forces

o Very low (or inexistent budget)

o Not destined to the professional (prevailing market culture) set-up

Trusted & trustworthy

Authentic, Organically grows Has a clear identity

o o o who it is, what it does & what is its story

It is okay if things are not perfect

The personal and professional spheres merge

Active on social media (one or several platforms)

Revives "older" or forgotten types of skills

Grow to standardizing or unifying appearances on social media and other communications channels
- Photo style
- Video style
- Visual codes/design codes

Figure 3.3 The personal fashion brand

o Grow and enhance
  what you have

o Aim at presenting
  a better version

Transforming
passion into business?
Or keeping passion as
a business?

Is it "anti-consumerism"?
Is it the appreciation of "the now",
"the slow" & "the cool"?

o o o

Born on social media
Fed by social media

- Has to stay true
- Could collaborate or work on partnerships
- Could grow into alternative distributions
and communications channels

Auto-motivated
Aims at showing
constant improvement

React and interact with
audiences (actively
listening to what
audiences are asking for)

The brand's value lies in its
ability to reach greater
audiences on social media
platforms and sites

An engaged
following

Frequency and style of
appearances and the
extent to which the style
is conversational

mentors who have been in the field for long will elevate in the business in no time. However, when newborn brands have no expertise or guidance, they are more likely to struggle and face many uncertain situations.

- No business can grow in isolation; the network lays the operations debuts, constructs and strengthens member relationships. Network members become newborn brand collaborators.

- The start-up capital: this capital is the sum of know-how, knowledge, suppliers, access to the market's infrastructure, financial capability (own investment or looking for investment) and so on. It is the newborn brand's energy source that will fuel up its engine. Capital has no value if it is not channeled or guided. Newborn brand founders must delicately balance their decisions in a way that the capital's consumptions transform into fruitful outcomes. What newborn brands need is to put their capital at the benefit of their business model until it becomes operational.

- The founding team members: fashion retail is about people. People who believe in the newborn brand's idea, who abide by its philosophy and who can share it, with the same passion and drive, with other members of the community. Team members must associate their talents and skills to meet the newborn brand's needs.

A newborn brand's timing contributes to the concept's acceptability. Consumers must find a true value in what the brand has to offer at this moment in time. Therefore, understanding the retail environment is a must; the brand's founder and team should assess the product's relevancy and the extent to which it is going to be accepted. Keeping an eye open, lending an ear to customers, exchanging with network members and evaluating own actions helps newborn brands steadily grow.

With a clear brand identity and all brand elements in order, newborn fashion brands need to communicate a narrative and to integrate it through all its touchpoints: in its physical store, online store, social media sites or any other platforms/channels it decides to adopt. Building a strong sense of belonging to the brand's universe strengthens the brand's community and relationships between community members. Newborn brands accompany consumers in their daily lives. They grow as they grow; they learn from them and try to always find solutions for them. Together, they mature into a building a strong relationship that goes beyond a mere transactional aspect.

Customers are at the heart of the great majority of today's newborn brand's business models. Whether at a product development level, a distributions level, a communications level or any other business level, newborn brands think of their decision's implications on customer decision-making and behaviors. They are more aware that customers request more transparency concerning each step involving the offering: conception, sourcing, material, process of production, country of production, legal aspects, communications, distribution to personnel or team members. On one hand, newborn brand offerings are inspired by the customers, and developed to meet customer need. On the other hand, customers access to the brand's offering would be the result of a meaningful act of consumption.

Together with customers, newborn brands actively participate in making the fashion retail environment a better place. As customers have become more conscious and have access to information, they are influencing brands into becoming more responsible in their decisions as well. With regards to the fashion retail environment, many changes took places, whether at the level of the offering, business models or types of businesses. The prevailing market mindset is that of transparency, traceability, sustainability, circularity and the fashion footprint (and those are only a few examples).

Coupling ongoing market watch with customer conversation helps in having an in-depth reading of the retail environment. Instead of taking decisions that are only based on traditional marketing tools and competitive analysis, newborn brands invest in the conversation. They listen to what is important and deliver what matters the most. Newborn brands are comfortable with technologies, digital tools and recent retail advancements. They have an edge over other, more established, brands with operating these tools. At a communications level, for instance, newborn brands have a greater tendency to adopt social media platforms to communicate, promote and get in touch with customers. They are comfortable with e-commerce, mobile and social commerce.

What newborn brands significantly invest in, is physical retail. Even if they lack financial resources, necessary to investing in traditional physical retail formats, newborn brands are leaning toward alternative physical retail formats. One of the adopted retail formats is pop-up stores. Another option can be that of participation in seasonal manifestations, multi-brand stores or private off-the-high street apartments. Finally, newborn brands could look at the option of a concession within locations that are attractive, beneficial in terms of footfall, visibility or others. Physical formats are digitalized, link with other digital platforms and social media platforms. Newborn brands and their community are accustomed to the extension of a physical sphere onto digital spheres; they are also technologically savvy and acquainted with different forms of online and offline shopping.

The newborn brand's sphere, which merges online and online spheres, unifies its community. It informs, narrates, amazes, delights, shares, receives and gives back. What better than physical retail to gather the community? What better than physical retail to keep the conversation going? What better than physical retail to engage with customer and give customers room to engage with the brand?

Newborn brand   Initial investment (necessary?)

Newborn brand type

                                     Clear on what the brand
Product/service brand   wants to do? Achieve?

Nomad brand   Structured? Unstructured?

Me brand   Planned? Accidental?

                                     Trial and error? Organic?
Opportune brand
                                     Testing and retesting?
Come-together brand

Is the brand relevant?   o o o   "Shaping phase"
Is the brand delivering
differently and putting   o Actively enhancing the work
heart into the process?   process
                                     o Actively listening to consumers
                                      and stakeholders
                                     o Making amendments and
o Is the brand's concept relevant?   refining the work process
o How will it do better?
o Why should community members
  (customers) believe in the brand?
o Why should they support it?
o What types of needs of the brand
  fulfill?

                                Is the customer at the heart of the brand?
                                -   What can the brand do to meet its
                                community?
                                -   What is the brand doing to do to meet
                                its community? (literally)

[Finances]

A backwards calculations method

Working with what the brand has/ has access to   Possible checklist
Are there going to be sufficient funds to test,
develop or mature a concept?
Are there ways to access to funds?

Figure 3.4 The newborn fashion brand

Thinking of the concept
Having a clear identity
Small does is not unprofessional
Visibility does not imply professionalism

[Starter Kit]

Brand's concept/ brand's ethos
Visual identity elements (and translating into all brand touchpoints)
Unified tone of voice (internally, with stakeholders, offline, online)

Brand's sphere
An office, an atelier, a co-working space, a laptop, a showroom, a stockroom (…)

[Social relationship]

[Social relationship becoming transactional?]

How much time does the brand need?
How much time does the brand have?
What does the brand need to speed up the process?
Does the brand have what it takes to speed up the process?
Is the brand convincing the community? Will the community engage in the brand's offering?

o Business detailed description/narrative
o Estimation of elements that are needed to make the narrative a reality
o Moving backwards: what is the brand selling? (Emotional value, market value, cost price, retail price)
o What profit margins? Threshold insuring brand's stability and potential growth?

o How many units to be sold, at what prices, during which period of time?
o The time needed to knit community relationships and consistently communicate the brand?
o What is the cost of referrals, community support? At what cost?
  All costs related to delivering the offering (end-to-end)

Mature fashion brands

Confronted to a new fashion retail market reality, mature brands could face a great threat. Shall they fail to cope up with change, their identities and concepts might get diluted, thus putting the very brand at risk. Mature fashion brands cannot let their guards down and should be on a 360-degree watch. They must undertake that they believe helps the brand. If start-up brands struggle with finding stability and growth, mature brands struggle with finding ways to reinventing themselves to stay relevant and true. Which mature brands are those more likely to dilute?

- Failing to reposition a product brand: product brands face greater challenges if their models are forged to deliver that offering. The product marketing concept finds no place on today's market, as the product is no longer a competitive advantage nor a relevant selling proposition. Moreover, the selling concept is no longer a valid or relevant proposition. Mature brands are to rethink their proposition and its value to customers.
- Brands that failed to extend their offering: Brand tend to extend their offering when their product's consumption become less relevant or less recurrent. Failing to extend the offering limits the brand's chances of serving its current customer or potential customers.
- Brands that failed to augment their offering: when products have become easily reproduceable, their features no longer an attractive selling point, or them being easily replaceable by those of the competition, brands must augment their offering. It is only normal that mature brands rethink not only their product's enhancements, but how the total product stands before consumers.
- Brands that did not invest in their customers: long gone are the days when brands impose or force their product on the market and audience. Those brands that did not put the customer at the heart of their strategy will see themselves drifting away from the fashion retail market. Customers who don't see a meaningful connection with a brand will no longer feel the urge to interact with it or spend at it.
- Brands that did not get on the digital sphere: different brands have many available distributions and communications tools and platforms to choose from. With the past decade's eruption of electronic and mobile commerce and social media communications, adopting one or more of these tools was inevitable. In an omnichannel retail context, it is crucial to adopt tools that ensure the brand's presence online and offline, and customer journeys within these touchpoints. Mature brands invited pick those tools that best meet with their identities.
- Brands that did not want to be transparent or ethical: customers have become informed, aware and demanding. Many want to be assured that their relationship with the brand is aligned with their personal set of beliefs.

Furthermore, they claim knowing about the brand's practices in developing the product and the sources with which that product was developed. At a services level, they are much concerned with all internal management practices. Consumers also look the mature brand's engagement with the retail environment and the extent to which its actions have a positive impact on it.

- Brands that failed to follow up on the fashion retail environment's market trends: whether market and consumer related trends, product trends, production trends or marketing and communications trends, brands have a lot of information to process. Considering the current fashion retail environment's happening, mature brands are to keep an open-eye and an open mind. Adopting change and adapting the brand's management to it is vital to its survival; all integrations or changes must be in line with the brand's identity.

Mature brands are to thrive for excellence in what they offer, how they offer it, how they communicate, how they deliver and, most importantly, how they keep their community at the heart of their actions. The size of the community requires considerable attention and considerable management; locally, nationwide or in any location that the brand operates in. Location is a significant strategic management element; local market, steeped culture, individual's habits or any other aspect reflecting a particular location is taken into consideration. Micro-management reflects the brand's willingness to involve its community in what it does.

At a local level, mature brands also look at ways of making their presence known. They take actions to enhance the local environment, such as investing in community schools or parks, renovating iconic budlings, investing in young talents or emerging or supporting local entrepreneurs. At a general brand level, mature brands keep communicating their brand with respect to all brand identity elements. Their discourses are clearer and include more transparency. Communications, online, offline or live, gives more space for customer expression with supervision and control.

During the past decades, brands have paid much attention to managing customer relations. Collecting customer information and data about them, their preferences and purchases, helped brands deliver the right offering. More recently, mature brands have been concerned with how to add value to that delivery. They are investing in physical retail environments to ignite engagement. To do so, it reimagines its physical touchpoints, and the ways they need to be designed, to make that engagement happen. With that management perspective, mature brands would know who their customers are, what they like what they expect and how they would expect to have that.

Reinventing the customer online and offline experience is necessary, if not central, to mature brands' survival on the fashion retail market. The customer is at the heart of managing experiences. Online, the brand invests in delivering a unique user experience. In-store and with other physical touchpoints, the brand invests in creating a space that delivers a unique customer shopping experience. Together with brand/customer active exchange, a holistic brand experience is co-created. Customers also have the possibility to share their opinions about that experience with other community members; whether online or offline. Mature fashion brands have rewarded their customers for their loyalty; a thank you letter, a discount or an exclusive preview. In addition to rewarding customers for their purchase, mature brands are rewarding customers for their engagement. Today's brand metrics could add to their *return on investments* and *return on experience* a *return on engagement*.

Newborn brands pay close attention to social and experiential dimensions. They experiment with new ideas, concepts, channels or formats. They rethink their physical store's atmospheric design, their online or virtual store's design. This process looks at the best ways to valorize a customer's contact with the space (offline or online), his contact with others and the access to the brand's offering. The prevailing fashion retail culture is conceiving spaces that revive the shopping experience: utilitarian spaces, immersive spaces, social spaces and interactive spaces. One mature fashion brand could rethink its retail touchpoints in a way that re-invents its customer journey's overall experience.

Keeping retail at the heart of fashion brands

Now that a fashion brand has seen, explored and endured enough in its environment, it will have to find a balance to be healthy and maintain healthy relationships with other society members. It will be thinking of all possibilities to manage it brand in the complex and turbulent, online, offline or alternative retail environment. This complexification requires a strong central management capable of guiding all brand activities. Any fashion brand operating in today's retail environment is exercises constant micro/macro management, fueled by its ethos and directed toward its customers.

Staying true to the (fashion) brand's identity is as important as keeping the brand at the heart and mind of consumers. Brands are to keep an ongoing conversation with customers and consumers to understand their motives, decipherer their intentions, anticipate their needs, answer their questions or listen to what they have to say. A physical touch point would always be the best option; it makes it possible for the brand to physically meet with customers and for customers to meet with the brand and other brand community members. With its ability to transfer non-verbal brand messages, the physical touch point encapsulates all design elements of the (fashion) brand. The space's conception is evidence of the brand's persona, its history and story. Today's fashion retail physical touchpoints, whether permanent or ephemeral, revive a human connection and nurture it to become a lasting relationship.

A physical touchpoint is an integral member of all other touchpoints representing the brand; it adopts a specific format, serves a function for a determined, or undetermined, period. Whether to facilitate the access to the

Table 3.1 The physical fashion retail brand's triad

Physical fashion retail format	Function	Format	Duration
	– Transactional	– Typical	– Long-term
	– Experiential	– Atypical	– Temporary
	– Facilitator	– Combined	– Ephemeral
	What is it going to offer? Where does it stand vis-à-vis other brand channels?	Rethinking the physical retail's form to meet customer expectations	Staying, moving or keeping up a hyperactive retail model?
	⊕		
Non-physical fashion retail format	– Online [intermediary dimension] – Social media and social commerce [complementary and linking dimension] ⊕ – Metaverse [alternative retail dimension]		– Complete physical retail formats – Reproduce or repeat physical retail formats

brand's offering or to give customers the possibility to live a unique brand experience, the fashion retail format's function must be clear. Customers must understand the function of that retail format and how it stands vis-à-vis all other brand touchpoints. The choice of the fashion retail format supports its function and helps the brand translate its characteristics through the physical format's atmospheric dimensions. As retail life cycles and product life-cycles are paralleling the dynamic of customer consumption life cycles, the "duration" variable is not to neglect. The more permanent a physical store is, the more it requires reinvention. The shorter the physical store is lived, the more it requires support, affirmation and repetition. Non-physical or alternative retail formats can re-create most a brand's physical atmospheric elements. The fact that they are less capable of transferring the *human* criterion and not fully allowing the encapsulation of *human sensory elements* could be handicap to the most-valued conversational dimensions that fashion brands are now looking for.

Different (fashion) retail brands develop different fashion retail environments; besides, their atmospheric design stimulate different types of engagement. Conceiving physical (fashion) touchpoints considers six factors, each naturally reflecting a brand's positioning. The "feel" relates to the physical touchpoint's general ambiance and its influence on the individual's senses. The "look" is a design dimension that could be managed to meet the physical format's function. The "social" factor considers the individual's presence in each space. The "design" factor contributes to facilitating in-store social interaction and the extent to which that interaction is needed.

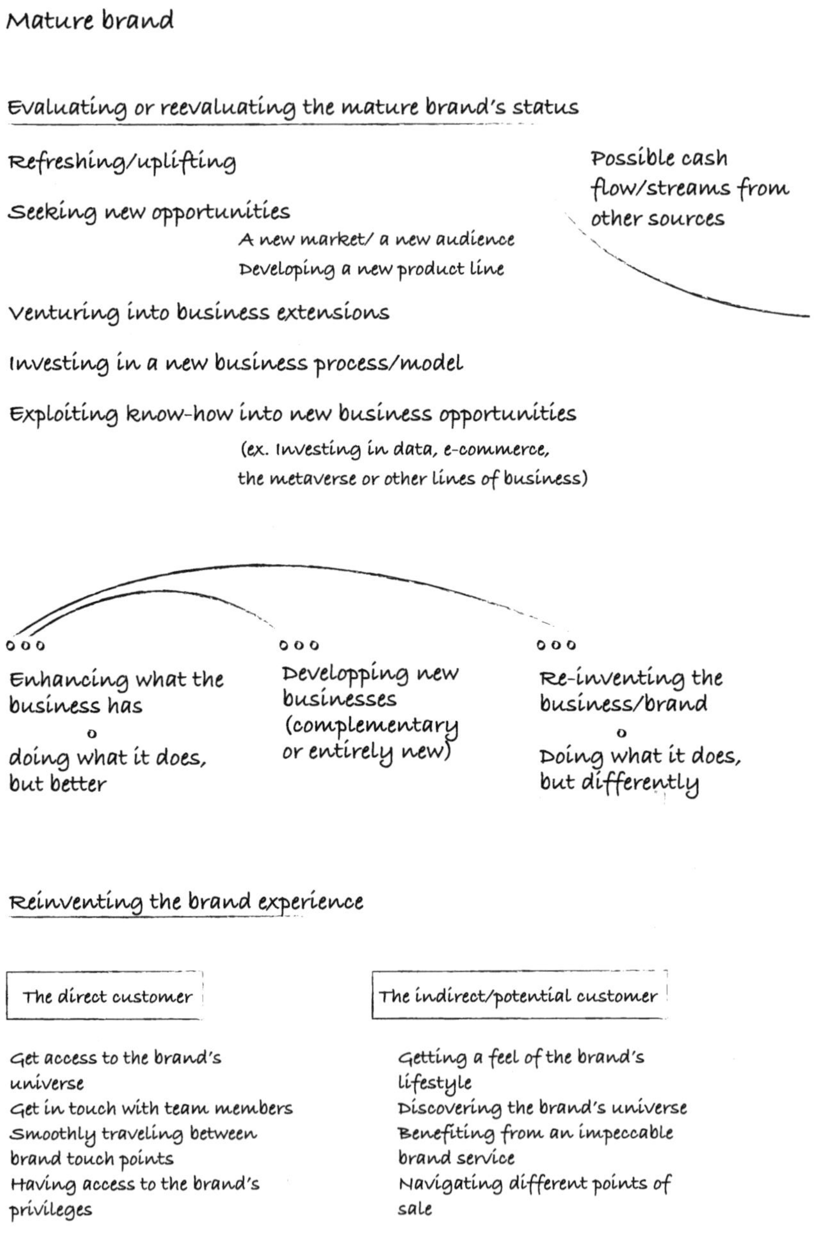

Mature brand

Evaluating or reevaluating the mature brand's status

Refreshing/uplifting

Seeking new opportunities

      A new market/ a new audience

      Developing a new product line

Venturing into business extensions

Investing in a new business process/model

Exploiting know-how into new business opportunities

      (ex. Investing in data, e-commerce,

      the metaverse or other lines of business)

Possible cash
flow/streams from
other sources

o o o

Enhancing what the
business has

o

doing what it does,
but better

o o o

Developping new
businesses
(complementary
or entirely new)

o o o

Re-inventing the
business/brand

o

Doing what it does,
but differently

Reinventing the brand experience

The direct customer

Get access to the brand's
universe
Get in touch with team members
Smoothly traveling between
brand touch points
Having access to the brand's
privileges

The indirect/potential customer

Getting a feel of the brand's
lifestyle
Discovering the brand's universe
Benefiting from an impeccable
brand service
Navigating different points of
sale

Figure 3.5 The mature fashion brand

o o o

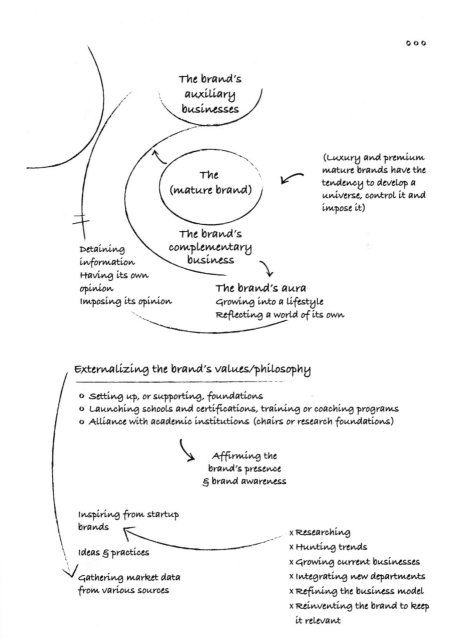

The brand's
auxiliary
businesses

The
(mature brand)

(Luxury and premium
mature brands have the
tendency to develop a
universe, control it and
impose it)

The brand's
complementary
business

Detaining
information
Having its own
opinion
Imposing its opinion

The brand's aura
Growing into a lifestyle
Reflecting a world of its own

Externalizing the brand's values/philosophy

o Setting up, or supporting, foundations
o Launching schools and certifications, training or coaching programs
o Alliance with academic institutions (chairs or research foundations)

Affirming the
brand's presence
& brand awareness

Inspiring from startup
brands

Ideas & practices

Gathering market data
from various sources

x Researching
x Hunting trends
x Growing current businesses
x Integrating new departments
x Refining the business model
x Reinventing the brand to keep
   it relevant

Table 3.2 Physical fashion retail brand atmospheric dimensions

Physical retail dimensions		Mass brands	Masstige brands	Lifestyle and premium brands	Luxury brands
Feel	Ambiance	Readable	Overwhelming	Mesmerizing	Transporting
Look	Design	Functional displaying	Product/offer staging	Product/offer allure	Exclusive access to the brand's universe
Culture, attendance, knowledge	Social	Self-service with on-demand information	Attention to customer	Attendance to customer's demands	Dedication to the customer
Community	Sociability	Accentuated on social media channels	The physical touchpoint is a place of expression	Community gathers in adapted environments	Impenetrable and inaccessible elite community
Increasing the brand's appeal	Services	Complementary and add competitive edge	Optional add-ons to differentiate an offering	Value creators	Integral and mandatory to maintaining brand standards
Dirven by store design and social media	Storytelling	Though physical touchpoint and online communications	Engaging	Immersive and participative	Sheltering in a themed environment with attention to minimal details

(With reference to Baker's typology (1982) and integrating factors highlighted from analyzing fashion brand cases that were intended for developing this manuscript.)

What is more important is that brands ignite the conversation and turn into an ongoing talk; the physical environment supports in strengthening the community and giving it a purpose. Designed to tell a story, the physical touch point becomes a vessel in which customers and brand representatives live a story. In some cases, the brand's offering could be an integral part of the narrative. In other cases, a passage through the store is necessary to collect information about the offering and collect it from other touchpoints. It is worth highlighting that the physical touchpoint's value is not restricted to its mere design; the more services it offers the better. A coffee shop, restaurant, an exhibition, an alteration service or any other complement that the brand sees fit, would elevate the brand and its touchpoints. In today's fashion retail environment, brands moved from presenting an augmented product to presenting an augmented touchpoint.

- A mass brand's physical touchpoint's atmosphere is more likely to focus on the offering in a way that it is clear and readable. Its display is functional as it intends to facilitate and accelerate the customer's visit to the store. No space is allocated to the brand's community; therefore, it tends to gather online, on social media platforms. In addition to social media communications, in-store communications disseminate information about the brand. As product differentiation becomes a farfetched objective, all services that the mass brand adds are indented to differentiate it from others.
- Masstige brands stage their offering in an overwhelming atmosphere. They pay attention to customers and attend to replying to their questions or filling in the requested information. The physical touchpoint is a place of expression where brand and customer flaunt their love for aesthetics and physical appearances. The touchpoint integrates design elements that engage customers and delight them.
- The design of premium brand physical points is mesmerizing and enchanting. With an immersive and participative design, customers are transported into the brand's world and blend in the environment only to become one with it. The brand's offering is presented with allure and poise; it will transfer its qualities to those who will acquire it. The premium brand's representatives are driven by excellence; together with the community, they share the passion around the offering and how it adds value to their lives.
- Luxury brands aim to give an exclusive access to its selected community; the physical touchpoint is a tight doorway to an enrapturing environment. An attention to detail at design, product and service levels elevates the brand. Community members are demanding and expect that the brand offers a dedicated service to them. The brand's community is impenetrable from the outside, yet, very engaged in the brand's universe from the inside.

In these turbulent times, fashion brand physical touchpoints keep the brand close to its community. They provide spaces for exchange and interaction and make room to receiving all those who want to come to the brand.

Finding clarity in the middle of the storm

Many questions are being raised by (fashion) brands: how can a *traditional* brand make sense in an unconventional market? How can a newborn brand make it "big" in a fierce retail environment or, how can a brand "draft its own rules" without becoming an "outlaw"? What is the fashion brand of "today"?

It looks like many retail market rules are being revised or reassessed; in the meantime, if a brand wants to survive, it must be relevant, it must be fit, it must be agile and it must adapt to change. There is no place for boring retail and brands need to keep that in mind.

Fashion brands have been operating under strict market rules; distribution formats, distribution strategies, physical store guidelines, merchandising guidelines, personnel and management processes and so on. Even if brands have been considered as "revolutionary" and different, what has been guiding the fashion retail environment for the past decades is changing. Brands must adapt to the turbulent retail environment and to customer fluctuant "consumption mood", and to adopt agile processes that allow them to survive these times and to stay true to their identities. Whether online, offline or temporary, fashion retail brands are invited to think of ways that make "more sense" to customers. Their retail formats are to be thought of as points of access to the brand's world, a transparent place of exchange or sharing and of co-creation.

Tired, confused, but hopeful

The past decade has been eventful, and retailers have been very much impacted by all the changes that took place. The fashion industry has seen better days; it is now confronted to a new reality that questions the very essence of fashion consumption. Do customers need as much as fashion brands are offering? are customers leaning toward minimalism? Are customers looking to allocate their fashion-related spending onto other types of spending? Is promoting mere fashion products still relevant? How could fashion brands integrate all trending retailing concepts?

DOI: 10.4324/9781003173212-5

One thing is for sure; the retail environment has changed, and fashion brands must do something about that. New technologies, practices, behaviors that occurred cannot be undone. Fashion brands would be less likely to survive if they look the other way. An unsettling retail environment affects different brand types in many ways. Whether they embrace change or deny it, (fashion) brands are going through the inevitable.

- **Deniability**: brands cannot deny the fact that online commerce, mobile commerce, social media have become integral elements of the retail environment. They cannot deny the fact that metaverse is taking shape and finding its spot next to other retail formats.
- **Plausibility**: (fashion) brands must reorganize, rethink or reintegrate formats into their current (or revised) business models. Fashion retail forms and functions are changing and that it now inevitable.
- **Plausible deniability**: (fashion) brands must assume that the fashion retail environment is witnessing an era of massive change and that many tools that have been available, have expired and are no longer valid.
- **Active anticipation**: It is crucial that (fashion) brands stay put and focused. Guided by a clear vision, they can anticipate or take actions that are necessary to keep the brand afloat during turbulent times.
- **Passive substitution**: during turbulent times, (fashion) brands might underestimate market realities. They might look the other way and pay less attention to changes that capable of threatening their business. Shall this happen, brands risk dissolution.

The yin and yang of fashion retail

There must be a positive side to all this confusion; it is all a matter of managerial perspective. Today's turbulent fashion environment calls of wise decision-making, finding a balanced state of keeping the ship afloat amidst the storm. When shore is at sight and managers will be capable to examine and evaluate it, they will then lead their ship and dock it at the most convenient spot. Given the retail environment's reality, a (fashion) retail brand's equilibrium affects short and long-term objectives, internal management processes, product, distribution and communications actions. Difficult to achieve, yet imperative to meet, finding the (fashion) brand's equilibrium requires a holistic assessment and approach. Knowing that each action has a direct effect on the brand, carful and informed decision-making is recommended.

As an active social actor of the fashion retail environments, a fashion brand is invited to find its equilibrium by looking several aspects:

- **Learning by unlearning**: the shelf life of many practices that fashion brands and retailers have acquired could have now reached its limits.

Newborn brands could unlearn faster than mature brands as they have not confirmed the adoption of a certain management process. Mature brand, however, could spend more time finding out how to "unlearn" and "relearn" while staying true to their identity and keeping their brand in a state of equilibrium.

- **Exploring and experimenting**: As the retail environment opens for new and different opportunities, brands are to explore them and take the time to experiment whether they are the best fit or not. Many retail formats, such as the ephemeral, give brands the possibility to experiment during a limited period. Such actions, if not repeated or anchored in space and time, will have no negative impact on the brand.
- before deciding to adopt or drop
- **Receiving and giving back**: contributing to the environment and society in which the brand lives in is as important as contributing to the brand's well-being. It is less likely that (fashion) brands survive in an unhealthy and tired entourage. Keeping in mind that every member of society must contribute to its well-being, (fashion) brands will only receive when they have contributed to something.
- **Collaborating**: in addition to a (fashion) brand's contributions, it could very much consolidate its efforts to supporting or meeting a defined, business or societal, objective.

Understanding "the now" and getting ready for tomorrow

There are no certainties to what will become of fashion brands or the fashion retail environment. One thing is for sure; change is upon us, and it has already begun showing its effects. Despite many speculations regarding the survival of fashion retailing, the relevancy of physical retail or the shifting interests of fashion consumers, there is hope. And the proof is that individuals are still consuming fashion. The proof is that there are still physical retail touchpoints. There is also evidence that customers do respond to change and that they like when it is relevant.

So how is retail really looking today?

- **Romantic** as it evokes feelings, sentiments
- **Relatable** to customers and individuals
- **Realistic** as it has become sensible and practical
- **Revitalizing**, re-energizing and bubbly

With respect to the fashion retail environment's realities, (fashion) brands are to carefully look at elements that need to be integrated at managerial and operational levels. All brand touchpoints, representing the brand momentarily or more permanently, must be congruent to its identity and helps it reach a perfect state of equilibrium.

- **The augmented physical store**: at times when augmenting the offering was a way to having a competitive advantage, today's (fashion) retail brands must augment their physical stores. Boring retail has no place in the fashion retail scene; it must create a greater value to customers and thus augmenting their experience. Physical retail's halo effect, on the overall brand's return on investment and experience, is key to its performance and success.
- **Direct customer contact. Direct sales**: re-investing in proximity retailing confirmed that physical retail remains an integral part of consumer's shopping journeys and that it responds to many of their shopping criteria, such as time and distance. There another "proximity" variable that retailers are paying attention to relational proximity. Getting into direct contact with customers, exchanging with them, meeting their expectations or simply being there for them is a winning investment for today's brands. customers who fail to relate to the brand's human side will not be motivated to keep any rapport with it.
- **Interaction**: the physical's retail format and online spheres, especially social media platforms, help in creating interactions with the brand and with other members of the brand's community. The physical store's atmosphere facilitates brand/customer interactions as it allocates a space for this to happen. All atmospheric elements are also welcoming and give customers the liberty to construct their experiences through in-store interactions.
- **From storytelling to story-living**: a (fashion) brand's physical environment become a space of immersion and interaction. Most importantly, it hosts individuals to take part of their world, to construct their experiences and become themselves the protagonists of the brand's story. The (fashion) brand's offering is an element of the story and could be accessed from the physical point or other brand touchpoints.
- **Entertainment, entertainment, entertainment**: as customers tend to get bored more easily, their attention directly shifts toward happenings that are novel, exciting and entertaining. The (fashion) brand needs to become a hub that continuously pumps life and dynamism. It has been more common for customers to make the effort to go meet the brands; more recently, brands are putting effort into coming themselves closer to the customers, even, to directly meet the customer.
- **Human brands**: with that perspective, fashion brands become relatable, approachable and personal.

Indeed, retail has become closer to the customer and closer to being his second home. Keeping the customer at the heart of all brand decision-making processes retail has become:

- Hyper-personalized
- Hyper-customized
- Hyper-social

Indeed, all (fashion) retail environmental happenings are giving us a headache that we must live with for a while. If there is a last piece of advice, to give to fashion brands, to help them move forward in "these turbulent times", it would be straightforward:

> Turbulence is here to stay. Change has only just begun and no brand will escape that.
> Despite all predictive tools, there are no certainties of what is yet to happen or how it will happen.
> Each brand must collect all elements and tools necessary for its survival.
> With all decisions taken, each brand must assess whether they are relevant to their community (changes in consumer habits, climate change, new ecosystem, changes in points of contact, and so on).

Ever since the invention of department stores by Aristide Boucicaut in 1852, "father" of modern trade, there were many changes at the surface of commerce, but not its principle. Commerce, or modern retail, is still an act of exchange between two parties. If we come to think about it, there were no fundamental changes since the beginning of the century and yet retail is welcoming the 3.0 version. There will be a new era for doing the same thing but doing it differently.

What is a creative business? What is a creative fashion brand or a creative retail format? Fashion brands' main objectives are to be creative. "Creativity" is bringing no invention to the fashion retail environment; it is revisiting style, refreshing concepts and reviving formats to fit modern times. Cyclicality is at the heart of the fashion retail environments dynamic and applies to all its levels: the offering, the retail's format, communications and distributions.

Fashion retail's "new temporalities" are a mixture of culture, ethnicity, diversity, sharing, collaborating, opening up to change, accepting disruption of all retail "geniuses" who know how to capture the air of time and transport retail to the future.

This "new future" and the change it suggests is already upon us. It is beautiful, exciting and scary, all at the same time. It speaks of slowing down and of speed. It speaks of innovations and only presents revisions . . . this future is happening "now" and happening in "places" that are connecting brands with customers, once again. Retail formats are at the heart of fashion retail and their future is being reflected in all the efforts and developments that are happening now.

Index

Printed in the United States
by Baker & Taylor Publisher Services